GOODNESS DISTORTED

GOODNESS DISTORTED

by

W. Norman Pittenger

King's College, Cambridge, and formerly Professor of Christian Apologetic
General Theological Seminary, New York

LONDON
A. R. MOWBRAY & CO LTD

© A. R. Mowbray & Co. Ltd. 1970
Printed in Great Britain at the Pitman Press, Bath

S B N 264 64512 X

First published in 1970

Contents

Preface

THIS book is in two parts—the first, and longer, deals with the question of evil, a question which every human being and every Christian believer must face. The second part is an attempt to 'take love seriously' as a criterion which Christians must employ when they seek to understand the great affirmations of their faith in God, in Christ, in man's 'redemption' (as we put it), in the meaning of the Christian Church, and in the possibility of 'growth in grace'.

The two topics are intimately related, since it is the fact of evil which presents our greatest obstacle to the conviction that love is indeed central in life and in the world, while the conviction that (in spite of all appearances to the contrary) love is thus central makes it possible for us to face evil and triumph over it. Hence it is not accidental that I have put the two parts together to make a single book.

The material on evil is a development of lectures which I gave in New York City for many years, as part of a 'required course' at the General Theological Seminary where for over thirty years I was first instructor and then professor of Christian apologetics. The second section, on love, comprises lectures which I was privileged to give to clergy of the diocese of St. Edmundsbury and Ipswich, in this country, in February 1969. I am indebted to Canon Churchill for the invitation to give the latter lectures, which were taken down on tape and then transcribed, so that I might prepare them for later publication.

King's College NORMAN PITTENGER
Cambridge

PART ONE

The Distortion

1

Introduction

IF anyone expects to find in this small book a detailed and complete study of what we commonly call 'the problem of evil', he will be greatly disappointed. Not only is such a study beyond my own abilities, which is obvious; it is also an impossibility on the face of it. Better men than I, certainly men much wiser than I, have lately attempted to deal with 'the problem of evil' and at the end have admitted that they have but scratched the surface. I think of two recent books, each of them admirable, which have concerned themselves with the subject: the late Austin Farrer's *Love Almighty and Ills Unlimited* and John Hick's *Evil and the Love of God*. They are excellent books, suggestive where they are not compelling; they seek to cover the ground as thoroughly as possible. Yet both writers are compelled to admit that in the last resort evil remains a surd and that it constitutes for them, as for all of us, the one really serious objection to faith in God as supremely good—in fact, as that 'love' which appears in both the titles.

When men like this make an admission of that sort, who am I to rush in with a supposed 'answer'? But I do not here attempt an answer. For I agree with Baron von Hügel, who told a correspondent (in a letter which afterward became one of the essays in *Essays and Addresses*) that Christianity does not have an *answer* to 'the problem of suffering' (and by extension, of evil), if by this one means a theoretical explanation of an unquestioned fact. What it does have, he said, is a practical way of dealing with suffering (and evil); this is demonstrated to us in the Cross of Jesus Christ, where 'the nettle of life' was grasped boldly, as he put it, where evil was neither denied nor explained away, nor accepted with Stoic indifference, but where it was somehow taken, absorbed, and transfigured. In the spirit of Jesus on Calvary, by identification with him and that spirit, the Christian claims, we too may deal with evil in a practical way.

What then are we trying to do in the present essay? Three things: first, to face the fact of evil as it is; second, to see it in the context of a view of the world which is both philosophically 'possible' and Christian; third, to consider what Calvary has to say to us about that fact and its overcoming in faith; and fourth and last, to make some suggestions about our own responsibility and opportunity in respect of evil. That is all; certainly it is all that *I* can attempt. And even then, what is said must be tentative rather than final.

The references just made, to Calvary and to God's way of dealing with evil, might suggest that we shall be concerned with the Christian doctrine of the Atonement. But while it is obvious that occasional comments may bring this doctrine (or rather, the fact in human experience of the God-man relationship to which the doctrine points) into the picture, it will not receive special attention. Neither shall we devote much space to what is called 'sin'—by which I mean the responsible choice by men of that which militates against their proper fulfilment as men and hence is contrary to the will of God for them. I believe that sin is not the most difficult problem in the whole complex of problems included in the term 'evil'.

Many have thought that it was; but so far as I can see, it is in certain ways the easiest of them all. Why is this?

I should claim that William Temple was almost right in telling us, in *Nature Man and God* (p. 366), that sin is so probable that it can hardly be conceived as not taking place. In the context, Temple is saying that if one grants both human freedom and God's way of 'creating the world' (as we put it) through evolutionary process, the likelihood of human choice of that which is not for man's own best good and his intended fulfilment of his potentialities in becoming and remaining human, is so high that it is to be expected.

Of course, many theologians have assumed that man is a static substance—'an individual substance of a rational nature'—rather than a 'becoming'. Furthermore, they have had a view of God which is more like a master of puppets who pulls strings than like a loving father who lets his children make mistakes because only in that way can they 'grow up'. God's control of the universe has been pictured as the sort of control which some sultan or dictator claims over his subjects. Of course his decisions are for the best good of his creatures, but they are his decisions and not the creatures'. When this view is held, sin becomes an almost insuperable problem. If God is the puppeteer, if man is a static entity, then why should any man or any group of men violate the divine will?

My contention is that this entire picture is wrong. Instead of man as a static entity, we should have man as a 'becoming' movement towards fulfilment. Instead of divine dictation, we should have God luring, enticing, inviting, soliciting his children towards their own best good—the actualisation of the purpose which is theirs by the fulfilled realisation of the potentialities given them.

Instead of God's will as an imposed *diktat*, we should have the urgent desire that everything shall freely choose that which is indeed for its best development: God's will is that man should become what in the divine intention he is, a free, responsible, and responding 'process'. Furthermore, instead of regarding each man as a discrete individual, we should see him in relationship with other men, with the whole human race, organic to the natural order, and hence both influencing and being influenced by everything and everyone else in history and in nature.

If one has a picture like that, free choices made by men in their finitude and with their inadequate knowledge will many times be choices that in the long run, often in the short run too, are 'wrong'—they are not for man's true development in the good; hence they are contrary to God's will for man. And when these choices have accumulated over the ages, with the consequences that follow from that organic inter-relationship (each man influenced and being influenced by others), the human situation inevitably will be such that inherited 'habits', actual conditions in which men live as generation succeeds generation, will be most seriously against the true good.

The term 'original sin' is a very unhappy one, since it implies that human nature is radically wrong. No Christian can believe that, if by 'radical' we mean 'in his roots'; surely for Christian faith, which sees God as himself good and as 'making' a good world, nothing of the sort can be possible. Yet the fact of experience to which the unhappy term points is present to us all—we live in that situation and we must face it as it is. So must God, if he is related to the world in the most intimate sense of identifying himself with it, not only by Incarnation but by the very fact of his creative action within it. The doctrine of the Atonement is a way of asserting that God has both lived in the human situation and also has faced it as it is; what is more, his living in it and facing it brings about new possibilities for men. The doctrine—or rather, the doctrines, for there have been many of them— is less important than the reality to which it points: the experienced truth that when men identify themselves, in their ongoing movement towards actualisation, with the love which is God-in-action, supremely in the total event of Jesus Christ, they find that they are enabled to make a 'fresh start', despite their situation. They sense deeply that they have been 'accepted', just as they are; that they are loved by God in their sin, even if that sin is displeasing to him. They are accepted, as persons in community; and being accepted, they are recipients of a power (which Christians call 'grace'—God's love in action, as Kenneth Kirk defined the term) which strengthens them towards the right fulfilment in terms of their true God.

All this is by way of being a digression, of course. But it was necessary to speak briefly of sin and atonement, in order to make it clear that I am not neglecting the facts about which they are concerned. If we do not discuss them in this essay, it is because our immediate interest is in evil in the other senses about which we shall write in the next chapter.

Another preliminary matter requires attention. This is what I should call the organic nature of the Christian faith. Once again, we shall not discuss the many details of that faith, since by no means all of them are relevant to our present concern. But that the Christian faith *is* organic seems to me obvious. It is impossible to isolate details in such a way that they are taken simply in and of themselves, without connections or relationships with other details. I do not suggest that the Christian faith is a complicated affair; on the contrary, I think it is very simple—it is 'available' to any man, not a highly sophisticated 'system of truth' which only the equally sophisticated can grasp. *Non in dialectica complacuit deo salvum facere populum suum*, St. Ambrose said. It is very simple, proclaiming God as love, love disclosed and active in the affairs of his world, initiating and preserving all good which his creatures freely decide for, signally manifest in act in the Man Jesus, known and communicated in a fellowship of which he is both Lord and centre.

But if the Christian faith is not complicated, it is complex, in that it is rich and all-embracing in its range and coverage. Everything in it hangs together—God, Christ, the Spirit, man, the Christian community, eucharistic worship, prayer, loving action in the world. The enterprise known as 'comparative religion' is nonsense; what ought to be in view is 'the comparative study of religions', as indeed is perhaps the intention of the other phrase when it is used by modern scholars. Each religion, each faith, whether it be Christianity or Buddhism, Islam or Hinduism, primitive or 'advanced' religion, insofar as it is 'positive'—that is, historically communicated through a tradition in a community—is knit together, internally consistent in greater or less degree. Thus it is absurd to single out some given belief and 'compare' it with the same type of belief in another religious culture. The whole context in which that given belief is found qualifies, modifies, influences, and largely determines, the belief in question. Many years ago, Evelyn Underhill (in a valuable essay found in *Essays Catholic and Missionary*) insisted that the 'study of religions' should be along such 'organic' lines. Nowadays most of the experts in the field have followed her advice, whether consciously or unconsciously.

But however this may be, Christian faith above all others has this organic quality. A Scottish theologian once wrote a book on 'the organic nature of Christian truth'; his point was the same as ours, but it might have been better had he spoken of 'Christian faith' rather than 'Christian truth'. A Christian, certainly, is sure that his faith is 'true'; but the use of the word might suggest to some that what is intended here is a specifically dogmatic structure—and in that case, honesty would compel us to recognise that there have been, and are, dogmatic assertions which are not organic to the whole but which have been appended or inserted into the total Christian reality, yet are in contradiction to the major stress of that reality. One instance is the conception of God as 'unmoved mover', in the sense of a non-relational (save logically) deity to whom the creation is so adjectival that it makes no fundamental difference to him. This conception is so frequently (indeed almost universally) present in dogmatic systems that its blatant contradiction of the basic Christian affirmation about God as love is often overlooked.

It is not in the dogmatic systems that Christianity's organic nature is to be found—or when it is, what is discovered is a strange composite of elements that do not hang together. Where it is to be found is in the faith itself—in the central proclamation and its properly drawn corollaries, and in the response in commitment and discernment which is the act of faith on the part of believers. The whole here does hang together. And when in a later chapter we shall talk about Christian faith, especially with reference to the 'model' of God which it presupposes and demands, the wholeness will be in mind even if not explicitly stated again and again.

Mention of this organic quality of Christian faith brings us to the last of our preliminary considerations. As we have seen, the wholeness includes response on the part of men; and that response is both in their commitment and the discernment which goes with it (obviously I am indebted here to Ian Ramsey's useful discussion in *Religious Language* and elsewhere) and in their own action which follows upon it. If Christianity claims to tell 'the truth', that truth can be known to men only as they 'do' it—'doing the truth' is a Johannine mode of asserting that 'truth' for Christians is not a matter of intellectual comprehension so much as it is a matter of grasping, being grasped, and acting upon the disclosure of how things really go in the world, beneath all surface appearances and in spite of all contrary indications. Nobody can really be a Christian unless he acts like a Christian—that is a too simple way of putting it, but it may succeed in making my point clear. Of course what one ought to say is that nobody can be in the way towards becoming a Christian—i.e., a man finding his fulfilment in love, which is to say 'in Christ', to use a Pauline phrase —unless as a matter of fact he is thus 'becoming', making real or actualising in his total response to life those attitudes, that stance, the essential reference, which in his existential situation is his to make.

This is why I find myself so much in agreement with Baron von Hügel in his remark about the Christian way of dealing with the fact of evil. There are important rational considerations which we must by no means permit ourselves to overlook or neglect; we shall be obliged to attend to them later on. But what is supremely Christian is the way in which evil is 'handled', faced, dealt with, and used.

Nor does this rest back upon obscurantism. It is not a matter of falling victim to the fallacy which J. S. Bezzant used to criticise: 'declaring the mystery too soon'. Evil is here; we know it is here. It must be seen for what it is, although it must not be exaggerated after the fashion of some of the total pessimists. Thomas Hardy's lines are relevant:

> 'If way to the better there be,
>   It exacts a full look at the worst'.

Having seen evil for what it is, we must see what can be said, rationally or intellectually, that may qualify it or intensify it or both. In other words, we must use our eyes and our heads in order to come to a better understanding of what it is that confronts us, what it is we are talking about.

In the end, though, we must deal with it in action. Here it is; this is what it is like; these are the several considerations necessary to understand what we are looking at: *then*, inevitably and inescapably, we are called upon to do something in respect to it. Precisely here the organic nature of Christian faith becomes crucial, quite literally crucial. What we do in respect to evil if we are Christians must be in accord with, tied up together with, hang together with, what as Christians we take to be our position. That position for a Christian is 'beneath the Cross of Jesus', as the old hymn says. Not only so; the Christian position is in the shadow of that Cross and it is also the position of one who has learned to bear the Cross for himself. For the Cross has relevance to more than human sin, although naturally it is that aspect of it which most vividly strikes us, being what we are. In some fashion, the Cross has to do not just with sin, but with evil—and with death as a summation of evil.

When I was a theological student, one of my teachers was a distinguished American theologian of the time, Dr. William Adams Brown. I recall his saying that Christian hymnody dwelt lovingly and devoutly with the Cross, but sometimes the more classical hymns did not penetrate quite so deeply as the so-called 'gospel hymns' of simple people. He cited for an example the hymn we have already mentioned: 'Beneath the shadow of the Cross, I fain would take my stand'. Yes, he said, that is very important. Then he went on to speak of 'In the Cross of Christ I glory', which stresses another aspect. He spoke of 'When I survey the wondrous Cross, where the young Prince of glory died' (as Isaac Watts originally wrote the words). That provided an even deeper insight, he said. He mentioned Venantius Fortunatus, 'God is reigning from the Tree'. That was in a way the most profound of them all—God in the Man Jesus demonstrating in act his victory of love over all sin, but also over all evil and over death itself.

But, said Dr. Brown, there is something else, which such great hymns of the tradition do not so often assert. What was that? he asked. His answer was a 'gospel hymn', which he quoted as follows: 'There's a cross for everyone/And there's a cross for me'. Did he not touch the very heart of the matter? I think so. I believe that in its organic nature Christian faith includes the sort of response which that simple hymn indicates. The only real answer to the presence of evil in the world is not at the intellectual level, for we are in no position to provide an adequate answer at that level, finite creatures that we are, ignorant men that we are. When we have done our best—and we *must* do our best, intellectually speaking —we have to learn to 'bear the Cross'. That is to say, to respond to life in this world as it is and as we honestly know it to be; and to respond to it in the fashion and through the spirit of him who hung on the Cross on one Good Friday, 'outside the city wall', in sheer acceptance and in sheer love.

2

The Fact of Evil

I HAVE always been amused by a limerick which years ago I came across and copied. It runs like this:

> 'God's plan had a happy beginning,
> But man ruined the picture by sinning.
> We trust that the story
> Will end in God's glory:
> At present, the other side's winning'.

In this book we shall not concern ourselves, save incidently, with sin; our attention will be given to evil in its other senses. So the limerick is not quite apt for our purposes, unless we change the word 'sin' or 'sinning' to some other word. But the point which the limerick makes is worth our considering—for however evil got into the world, it does seem to many an eye that it is the evil and not God's good 'plan' which is 'winning', although we may indeed 'trust that the story will end in God's glory'.

As we bring this study of evil to a close, we shall have occasion to show why it is that Christians, if no others, must commit themselves to that trust, that confidence, yes, that 'faith'—for it is a matter of our faith which is at stake here. But we shall not go very far in our consideration of the whole question unless we take an honest look at the evil that is so plainly part of the world in which we live and of our own human experience.

I wish to begin, therefore, by insisting on the reality of the fact of evil. It is no illusion, no human fancy; it is a fact. We shall get nowhere if we minimise the fact or try to evade its stark horror. Nor should any Christian wish to do this, since he above all others should be aware of the happenings, the accidents, the things, whatever they may be, which seem so contradictory to a belief in a God who is himself good and who wishes only the good of his whole creation. Indeed, in this sense, we might say that the Christian faith increases the horror of evil, apparent as that horror must also be to any observant man or woman.

Of course there have been religious faiths which have attempted to run away from evil. They have said that it is only in 'appearance', not in reality. They have used various arguments to make their case, one of them being the claim that phenomenal or wordly events are only very partially participant in what they style 'being'. If that is so, then they can say that while evil has the appearance of existing, in the fullest sense it does not do so at all. We can, and we should, escape from the phenomenal realm where evil is seen and raise ourselves into the realm of 'pure being', which is the real world, uncontaminated by anything that contradicts primal goodness.

There have also been Christians, as they would insist on describing themselves, who have dismissed evil as 'unreal'. In fact, the last century saw the appearance in the United States of a religious group whose main interest was in this denial of evil. For members of that group, still a powerful movement not only in North America but elsewhere in the world, evil is only in the mind of the man or woman who has failed to purify and cleanse himself so that he will be able not only to rise above what looks like evil but will be able to see that it is, in fact, only something that 'looks like' evil—it is not truly there at all.

Such a device falls by its own efforts, however. By saying that evil is only in our 'material minds', it has not removed the patent truth that many, if not most, people are in the situation where the evil is very real to them—and where they dislike it. Members of this religious cult themselves tell us that evil is pure 'fancy', pure 'imagination'. Even so, they regard such mistaken fancy or imagination as itself a bad thing—else they would not wish to 'cure' it. Another limerick suggests itself to me at this point.

> 'There was a faith-healer of Deal
> Who said that pain wasn't real:
> "Yet when I sit on a pin
> And it punctures my skin,
> I dislike what I fancy I feel."'

Precisely. The supposed solution of the problem offered by these cultists is no solution at all. At best it is a highly unrealistic and illogical attempt to evade what everybody knows; at worst it is sheer escapism, with consequences that can be quite dreadful, as when a boy of my acquaintance died of peritonitis because his parents (members of the cult) refused to acknowledge that their son was suffering from an attack of severe appendicitis, hence declined to have a surgical operation performed, trusted to a so-called 'healer', and within a matter of days were mourning a much beloved, but now dead, child.

The sufficient comment on all this is in the lines of Thomas Hardy which I quoted in the opening chapter: 'If way to the better there be/It exacts a full look at the worst.'

On the other hand, as we shall point out, the authentic Christian attitude towards the world *is* ultimately optimistic. This is because it does not identify things as they are with God as he is, even if it finds God at work in the world and in those things as they are. When, for example, a father lamented the death of four sons from highway accidents in a town near Newark, in the United States, and said that he could not see 'why God has taken my boys this way' (I am quoting from an interview published some years ago in a newspaper), the Christian must demur from the implication that God is directly responsible for what happened. We shall concern ourselves with the questions which this must raise, but for the present my point is simply that evil is really there, inescapably known to us; it is not God's fault but somehow it is in the total scheme of things. Yet the faith of the Christian can see through the evil to a good conclusion of the matter. This does not reduce the horror about which we have spoken but it provides a certain perspective for us when we contemplate that horror.

If for the moment we exclude sin and what might be styled 'moral evil' in human experience from our listing of types of evil, the following might be a rough-and-ready sketch. There is evil in the natural world. There is suffering in the world of living creatures. There is suffering in human experience. These three types of evil should not be confused, yet it is true that they seem to belong together and it is quite clear that when most people talk of evil as such they intend one or other of these three.

Evil in the natural world is likely to face us with a problem. In just what sense, for example, is it proper to call a tidal wave an 'evil thing'? Or an earthquake?

Or a river-flood? In what sense can we say that a mosquito or a poisonous snake is 'evil'? To lump these together, along with other examples which come readily to mind, and then to speak of 'nature red in tooth and claw', while at the same time natural catastrophes are included in the general category, shows a remarkable failure in discrimination. It is understandable enough, to be sure, yet it ought to be plain that the human point-of-view is so central to such a picture that we are likely to get the matter out of proportion.

Some years ago, the then distinguished Harvard scientist L. J. Henderson wrote a book called *The Fitness of the Environment*. The scientific details in that once famous book may by now be out of date; but the main drive of Henderson's argument would seem to be impressive. He urges that as a matter of actual scientific knowledge, in the light of all that has been disclosed by the most careful study, the world in which we live is peculiarly adapted for the emergence and maintenance of something we treasure: namely, living matter, and more especially, human life itself. I am not competent to judge whether Henderson's contention will stand up to examination, but most of the scientists with whom I have talked have agreed that so far as they can see the conditions of the world have precisely that capacity to produce and to maintain life and human life. They have told me, for instance, that however dreadful may be an earthquake, it is so much part of the whole business of keeping this planet with a certain kind of temperature and with the preservation of what one of them styled 'the natural or physical *status quo*', that the occurrence of it from time to time, and usually in specific areas, is not a matter of regret.

What is more significant, so far as I can see, is that in

respect to this sort of natural evil, we only speak of it as such when there is a juxtaposition of the realm of physical change with the realm of living or human existence. A tidal wave which took place at some remote point in the Pacific Ocean, washing over an entirely uninhabited atoll, would not be regarded as evil; it would simply be accepted as 'a fact of nature'. But when there are people around, as we might put it, and when these people must suffer the consequences of the 'natural disaster', we are of course shocked and frightened and we cannot avoid calling the occurrence an 'evil thing'.

Such considerations might have a certain ameliorative quality, in that they indicate that evil in this physical sense is not a purely objective affair. The subjective participation of living agents, above all of those who are conscious and can be aware of what is going on, is very much a part of the scene. Indeed, in a more general sense, one must regard much of the talk about the 'objective', with no regard for the 'subjective', as fairly meaningless. One knows quite well what is intended, but it is or ought to be clear that whatever is called 'objective' is in fact being called that by a 'subject'. The supposition that one can split the world, and our experience of it, into the two regions or areas of the entirely 'objective' and the entirely 'subjective', rests back upon a simplistic epistemological attitude. Insofar as any objective reality is known to us, it has a subjective quality; insofar as subjectively we experience something, it is to that degree an objective reality—however mistaken may be our subjective evaluation.

There is a certain regularity about what goes on in the natural order. That order, to use a phrase of F. R. Tennant's, is 'relatively settled'. This does not exclude the possibility of new things; and its assertion should not be used as a way of denying that such new things actually have occurred and do occur. But the more or less intractable quality of nature, which has made it possible for science to study it, provides a kind of background for living matter and for human life. 'Background', perhaps, is the wrong term to employ here, since it may suggest that human life as well as animal and vegetable existence (as the old philosophers used to say) gets itself 'played out' on a stage which is alien in nature to such life. The fact would seem to be that nature itself is historical—that is, it is 'on the move' and is 'getting somewhere'. But about such questions we shall have something to say on a later page. For the moment, I am only interested in making the point that there is such a 'relatively settled order', in which our existence is set. That kind of order has made possible such scientific enquiry as has enriched both our knowledge and our daily life.

One of the quite practical corollaries of such regularity within limits is the possibility of prediction. Water always boils at a certain temperature; if it did not, there would be a complete uncertainty in respect to one whole aspect of life. If fire did not burn, it would not provide warmth. We very much dislike to have a finger burned, but we appreciate warmth during winter months. Through learning how properly to use fire, how to avoid the dangers which it may offer, and how to benefit from the good things that it can provide, human experience has greatly benefited. And this is but a single illustration, out of many that might be suggested, to show that the predictability of the natural order is a good thing which at the same time contains the evident possibility of something that we naturally will call bad.

Yet I should not wish to minimise the presence of those evil possibilities in the world of nature nor discount the obvious truth that when the possibilities are actualised we cannot fail to be disturbed. Why has not the world been made otherwise? Is it not at least conceivable that it might have been a place where nothing bad would happen at all, where all would be good and for our good? About such questions, one can only say that other conditions might have been, but that these are the conditions which we face. Such as it is, the world has to be accepted and we must do the best we can with it. We really have no choice in the matter. The *real* question is whether the world as it is can be regarded as in some sense the 'creation' of a good God, in which he is at work to accomplish ends or purposes that are also good. And that question is the one with which we are concerned in this book.

For myself, the most horrifying side of evil is in the suffering which I seem to see in the animal world. In that realm there is a sufficient degree of conscious awareness, with the development of the necessary apparatus of nerves, to make possible a kind of pain which I regard with more than dislike—I find myself appalled. But I realise that I may very well be guilty here of something like the 'pathetic fallacy'.

Here if anywhere nature does seem 'red in tooth and claw', with one animal preying on another, with death coming meaninglessly to a poor sentient creature, and with everything else that is so distressing to contemplate or to think about. Many years ago, my old friend and teacher Paul Elmer More, the American essayist and classical scholar, told me that he had once seen an horrifying incident near his summer-home on Lake

Champlain. A snake, of some sort, had managed to get to some other creature—I forget just what—and was engaged in slowly swallowing it, while the victim was undergoing terrible agony—or so it appeared to More. He said that it was the most horrifying spectacle he had ever watched; and there was nothing that he could do about it, since the snake was itself dangerous and the swallowing in any event had gone so far that the situation was irremediable. In that story, More was vividly stating my own sense of distress at this kind of animal suffering.

But when I told the story to a very eminent biologist, he charged me with being far too sentimental. According to him, the degree of actual suffering which was experienced was probably fairly minimal. He went on to tell me that on the whole suffering in the animal world is nothing like so severe as we might think it to be. We tend to put ourselves in the place of the creature in anguish and assume that its experience is identical with what we know our own would be in a similar case. But this is absurd, he said. Most animals which have developed a nervous system that enables them to feel pain (and pleasure too, for that matter) have not developed it to anything like the degree that obtains in our own bodies. And he insisted that the pain might be real but that it would be brief. He concluded by telling me that in his considered judgement life in the animal world is marked by a certain 'mild euphoria' (his own words), that suffering is not aggravated very much by what happens, and that death when it comes is not the long-drawn and painful experience which we might think it to be.

But once again I should insist that such considerations as my biologist friend adduced must not bring us to disregard pain in the animal world. It is there; and however minimal may be the amount of actual suffering in any given instance, we dare not talk as if it were unimportant. Thoughts such as this have been much in my own mind when I read about those who engage in animal hunting or other forms of unnecessary slaughter of what they call 'wild-life'. The eating of animal flesh, such as beef, is very pleasant; there is no need for us to be vegetarians. But there *is* need for us to make sure that no needless pain is inflicted on any beast, that 'slaughter-houses' are run efficiently and that the death which is inflicted in them is swift and 'merciful' in manner of execution, and that nobody engage in activities which increase the amount of suffering that there is in the animal world. 'Blood sports' seem to me to be a barbarous pursuit for civilised men. In saying this I realise how unpopular such sentiments may make me; but I should wish to urge that responsibility for the animal creation belongs to man to a very large degree and that man ought not to engage in any killing, or any activity leading up to killing, or any mode of entertainment in hunting and the like, which fails to see that responsibility and act upon it. The fox does not like to be hunted, nor does the hare. Talk of that sort is silly.

This is by the way, of course, rather than the main point which I am seeking to make. I wish to include in the category of evil the suffering in the animal kingdom and I wish to see that suffering as it is, without maximising it beyond the facts yet without seeking to find excuses for it. It is there and must be accepted as being there.

Perhaps because we are much more familiar with ourselves and with our physical constitution, we are prepared to recognise suffering in the human realm and we refuse to find any alibi for it. Such suffering is both physical, in the pains of the body, and mental or emotional, in the pains of the mind and feelings. Of course these are closely related, since man is a psycho-physical organism, his body affecting his mind and feelings, and his feelings and thoughts affecting his body. It is important, too, to remember that each and every man is bound together with his fellows, so that what they experience affects him, and vice-versa. A very large amount of the suffering which we know in the realm of human experience comes from our deep participation in this common life with others, above all with those for whom we deeply care.

It is not necessary to enumerate the various types of human suffering, beyond the mention of disease and illness—some of this quite terrible, as with cancer, the fact of death, which can be peaceful and undisturbed or can be very terrible too, and the many sorts of emotional and mental illness which appear to increase as the race becomes more civilised and hence more sensitive. Only the bigots or the blind can deny these various types of human suffering. They too are there.

One consideration which needs to be borne in mind, however, is that the very same conditions, physically, nervously, emotionally, and mentally, which make it possible for us to suffer in different ways, also make it possible for us to have a sense of enjoyment, happiness, and contentment. It has often been pointed out that the man who would wish to destroy all chance of experiencing pain must at the same moment deny all chance of experiencing pleasure. The organism which in its wholeness makes possible the one, of which we approve, also makes possible the other, of which we disapprove. That is the way things are. We might desire that they were otherwise, but we cannot change them. I once wrote that the 'equipment which is ours as men is the condition of our joy and of our anguish' and went on to say that 'a less sensitive creature than man, one less highly developed, one without sympathetic nervous systems, one without the social solidarity which is ours, might experience less pain or perhaps even none at all, but he would also diminish if not destroy his opportunity to find joy in himself and with other persons'. I see no reason to change that judgement.

So far in this chapter I have spoken of the evil which we seem to see in the natural order, especially (perhaps solely) when it has its bearing upon human existence. I have spoken of the pain which is known, with whatever degree of intensity there may be, in the realm of the animal world. And I have spoken of the suffering which seems inescapable in human experience. And I have tried to make it clear that while there are, in each of these instances, ameliorating considerations which must be kept in mind unless we are to see the matter entirely out of proportion to the reality, we are compelled to accept the fact of evil as it is.

But it would be wrong to forget that even in a study which is not specifically concerned with human sin or with moral evil, some account should be taken of the way in which wrong decisions by men, accumulating through the ages, along with irresponsible and careless actions by men in every period of history known to us, have had their very large part to play in bringing about certain evils which all of us would decry. The notion that 'sin is responsible for all evil', as I have heard it stated, would not seem to be true; but most certainly it is true that a good deal of evil could have been avoided if men had acted differently, had made different choices, and had been aware of their responsibilities.

It is preposterous to build houses in places known to be subject to earthquakes or where they are likely to suffer from floods. At one time this may not have been so, but thoughtful people would agree that when the knowledge is available it is irresponsible to risk any such enterprise. So also a fair amount of pain inflicted on animals is done by men. Nor can there be any doubt that better diet, more careful living habits, and the like, would diminish a certain amount of human suffering although by no means all of it. Whatever may have been the case in other ages, we have knowledge today about such matters, or at least a considerable increase in the partial information available; it is irresponsible to fail to act upon that knowledge.

This brings us to a very serious question. What is man and how can he best live his life?

It is easy to talk as if human life were best lived when everything is comfortable and pleasant. But most of us realise that not only is this impossible for us; it is also likely to contribute to a weakening of human fibre and a lessening of our true manhood. The man who lives a soft life becomes a soft person; there is a certain stiffening, hardening, life-enhancing quality about the experiences which bring us face-to-face with difficulties. When John Masefield wrote that 'the days that make us happy are the days that make us wise', he stated but half of the truth. Happiness may, indeed does, bring wisdom; but much of the time it is through our less agreeable experiences that we learn to become true men. To say this sounds like all those intolerable people who speak about self-imposed hardships as a way to develop character; but that is not my intention. I am only pointing out, what is indeed obvious, that what Browning called life's 'rebuffs' are one of the ways in which human life is enhanced and strengthened. In other words, life neither is, nor would most of us wish it to be, nothing but 'a bed of roses'— and even roses have thorns which can prick and hurt!

It seems to me that whatever else we may wish to say about the world as we experience it, we must acknowledge that it is a bracing place to live. It is not necessary to adopt a foolishly Stoic attitude, neither is it right to do anything to increase the hardships already present. But if the world looks and feels, in so many ways, 'like a battle'—in William James's phrase—it has managed to produce many noble men and women. Perhaps that is the sort of world which is best for us all, where we must take our chances, live with a certain degree of risk, face hardships, know pain, see evil as present and to be fought, and in this fashion make ourselves men.

I believe that something like this can be said. But I also believe that it can be said meaningfully only in the context of a more general world-view, however reached, which will provide a meaning for our lives and a meaning for the world itself. That is why we shall turn in the next chapter to a consideration of the sort of world which ours may be—the sort which I myself, at any rate, think is the case. This will require that we endeavour to work out a philosophical conceptuality which will take account of the facts, so far as we know them. For me, that conceptuality has been provided by the thinkers who have taken with utmost seriousness the evolutionary nature of the creation and who have used that perspective as a base for their understanding of 'how things go'—not only in the natural order, but in human history and in the realm of human experience.

3

Looking at the World

ONE would suppose that every informed and thoughtful person in civilised countries today takes for granted the evolutionary picture of the world. The fact that a hundred years and more have passed since the controversy over biological evolution, and that so much water has flowed under the bridge, makes it seem almost old-fashioned even to remark on this acceptance. 'We are all evolutionists nowadays', we might say. The days when the ordinary person believed that the acceptance of the evolutionary picture conflicted with the profession of Christian faith are long past.

If this is the case with the general population, it is more certainly true of theologians, save for the unimportant few who are associated with the various 'fundamentalist' sects. Even in the Roman Catholic Church, where there was considerable resistance for a time, contemporary theologians simply assume the truth of the evolutionary way of seeing the world. It is recognised that there is no essential conflict between that attitude and Catholic dogma as a whole, even if in certain specific areas (such as whether one accepts a monogenetic or polygenetic view of man's origin) there are still controversial discussions.

Yet this general acceptance of the evolutionary perspective, on the part of theologians of all types, has not always led to a re-conception of aspects of Christian belief which presuppose a more static way of looking at the world. If the creation is in process of evolution, if change takes place however slowly in the whole world-order, if the 'nature' of anything must be determined by its development rather than by some instantaneous *fiat* at the moment of 'first' creation, it is obvious that Christian thinking about the meaning of ideas like the creation itself, its characteristic qualities, and so forth, must undergo some very serious modification. When it comes to our thinking about what human existence is like and how it may best be understood, the evolutionary perspective once again demands a change from the older and more static notions that have been taken for granted in traditional Christian theology.

It is odd that theologians sometimes work as if one might accept the newer world-view and yet retain the old conceptions unchanged or only very slightly altered. When to this we add that these theologians are aware of the type of material found in the Book of Genesis in the Old Testament, knowing very well the mythical nature of the stories of the creation (both of them, for there are two there), the account of Adam's temptation and 'fall', and the resultant situation which classical Christian theology has called by the name 'original sin', one would have thought that they would have seen that this material can no longer be used as if it were revealed data for the development of a doctrine of creation, of man, of man's 'original righteousness', of man's 'fall' from that state, and of the resultant 'state' of sin in which the human race finds itself. Only a few decades ago, the distinguished Oxford theologian N. P. Williams was quite prepared to accept the evolutionary perspective, yet attempted in his large work on *The Doctrines of the Fall and Original Sin*, to retain the biblical picture as it had been worked out in classical thought, although from what he says explicitly in that book he was by no means uninformed about the position in respect to Old Testament study and what it has to tell us about the material which the Church Fathers inevitably used for their own statement of such matters.

On the other hand, it is right to say that most theologians in more recent years have been conscious of their obligation to do something about all this. In an Anglican thinker like William Temple, for example, we find just this; and whatever else may be imperfect about a work like *Nature Man and God* it cannot be faulted in this respect. Yet an equally distinguished theologian, Lionel S. Thornton, who both accepted and sought to use evolutionary ideas (and especially the organismic evolutionism of Alfred North Whitehead, to which we shall return), drew back when he came to the question of the person of Christ—although he did not feel it necessary to make this withdrawal in the case of man's nature as such. Thornton's refusal to apply the concepts which he drew from Whitehead, to the person of Christ will serve, however, as an illustration of a certain hesitation on the part of theologians to carry out their job completely in the new terms. And it is just this with which we are here concerned.

So far as our subject in this book goes a good deal of the specifically theological problem of evil is seen at exactly this point. If we continue to think of the creation as somehow a completed thing, which 'came into existence' at a given moment, the presence of evil in that creation becomes an almost intolerable difficulty, theologically speaking. Even if an evolutionary view is taken, it is still possible to think and talk as if the creation were simply there, in a relatively finished form. It is the great merit of the two books to which reference was made in the first

chapter (John Hick's and Austin Farrer's) that they do
not fall victim to any such error. Both of these books
accept quite fully and frankly the evolutionary point-of-
view; both of them find that the material in Genesis is
to be interpreted as an ancient way of speaking, in a
mythological fashion, of the dependence of the creation
upon its creative principle, rather than an account of
'what happened' which must somehow be reconciled
with evolution. Hence they are able to talk sensibly
about evil, as those who persist in a more static view
cannot do.

What I wish to suggest is that the world is not already
made; rather, it is a world still in the making. The
doctrine of creation, then, is a doctrine which has to do
with relationships between God, as chief creative principle,
and that which is not God ('the creation') but in which
God is unceasingly at work to elicit emergent levels
(call these what you will) through which his ungoing
creative purpose may be more adequately effected.
Very likely most theologians would agree—indeed it may
be recalled that St. Thomas Aquinas himself regarded
the doctrine in this way and accepted a moment of creation
at a point in time only because he believed that this was
taught explicitly in Scripture which naturally he was
obliged to take in a literal (or quasi-literal) sense.

But the difficulty with Aquinas' way of stating creation
as a relationship is a difficulty which in a different form
is also found in contemporary thinkers like Hick and
Farrer. Their view of God requires that they see him as
absolute and for them this posits an essentially one-way
relationship between God and the world—despite the
many places where they show that they are troubled by
this idea. What I mean is that a conception of God as

absolute, in the classical interpretation of such 'absolute-ness', suggests that while God is 'at work' in the world, and while in Christian faith he must be seen as loving and caring for his world, participant in its life, and sharing in both its joy and its pain, he is not affected by that world in the most serious way. To put it very simply, and far too simply to be entirely satisfactory, I would urge that God is working in his world in a manner which includes the overcoming of obstacles presented to him by the presence of something which is open to his action but may be recalcitrant to that action by reason of its own decision to seek actualisation in this or that (but not in every) occasion in terms of selfishly satisfactory ends rather than in terms of those ends that are for the greatest shared good. I should be prepared to say that the non-God world has a radical freedom which God himself must and does accept. That is how things are; and theologically we might phrase it by saying that such is how God wants things to be. His accomplishments in the world, with the ultimate victory of his good over everything, are to be achieved not by denial of but through those decisions in freedom. Because this is how things are, the working 'through decisions in freedom' requires a subtlety of divine operation rather than a direct and immediate manipulation of created or creaturely occasions.

In practice this means that God's way of working in the world is through his luring it, enticing it, inviting it, soliciting it, to respond in such a fashion that his purpose of good is achieved. At the same time, when an occasion does conform to the divine purpose, it also actualises its own best good. There is no radical contradiction between these two; God's purpose and the creaturely

satisfaction are identical. On the other hand, the very
fact of creaturely finitude presents obstacles to that fulfilment, while at the level of conscious moral choice the
decision may very well, and often observably is, against
the true fulfilment of the creature and hence against the
accomplishment of the divine purpose in the creature.
To assume that nothing of this sort can and does happen,
would be at the same time to deny the radical nature of
the freedom which is found in the creaturely occasions.

The preceding discussion will prepare us for a more
extended presentation of the way of looking at the world
which, as I believe, follows from a serious acceptance of
evolutionary fact and from the analysis of what it feels
like to be a created occasion in an evolving world. In
other words, I shall now outline a philosophy of process,
following (for the most part) the insights of Alfred North
Whitehead, to whom I have already referred, and those
of Charles Hartshorne and other thinkers of the same
school. Nor should it be forgotten that in a general way
these insights are also to be found in the work of the
French Jesuit palaeontologist Pierre Teilhard de Chardin.
But instead of reproducing the thought of any of these
men, I shall seek to give the main elements in this philosophical conceptuality in my own terms and as a Christian
theologian. I say this because I should not wish the reader
to assume that what I am about to write represents some
sort of agreed view, shared in its details by all process
thinkers; at best, it is my own way of seeing the matter
and only I can be held responsible for its deficiencies.
Furthermore, I may refer the reader to a more extended
discussion in my Cambridge and Sewanee lectures,
published under the title *Process-Thought and Christian
Faith* (London and New York, 1968).

To take with utmost seriousness the evolutionary perspective means that we must see everything as in process of becoming, rather than in terms of static given entities. Something *is* what it is *coming to be*—there is a dynamic and active quality about things. Nothing remains fixed, so that it may be looked at and analysed in the fashion in which we try to observe dead specimens in a museum or in a laboratory. Anything living is alive, we might say; and to be alive is to be changing, to be 'in process'. Even that which is 'dead' is not for that reason inert; a corpse is in process of corruption. A stick or stone is not just a given thing; it is an astonishingly complex series of physical changes. From the tiniest particles—call them electrical charges, if you wish—up to the greatest of the stars, there are combinations, re-combinations, alterations in pattern, appearance of novel configurations—this is how the world goes. Such a scientific picture is confirmed in our own experience of what it means to be a living human being—we too, as we know very well if we engage in a little introspective thought about what it 'feels like' to be human, are becoming, for better or for worse.

Process thought takes this point and moves on from there to a world-view which is in accordance with this fact of observation and this deliverance of introspection. But it is not only a matter of being 'in process'. It is also a matter of participation or sharing. The created order is a social process. In ways that may be infinitesimal what goes on in one specific occurrence has its affects in what goes on elsewhere. There are no walls of separation, so that we can contain and confine any given occasion and study it as if it had no relationship with anything else. This mutual inter-penetration is confirmed in physical science and it is witnessed by our own deepest awareness

of the way in which what we do, what we are becoming,
influences others as they influence us by their own doing
and becoming. This is why Whitehead and Hartshorne
have spoken about the 'organismic' or 'societal' nature of
reality. It is why Teilhard insisted so strongly upon
the inter-connections of everything in the creation.

It is true, of course, that for purposes of examination
and partial description, we may abstract any given occasion from the others. But the result of our doing this is
precisely what the word indicates: we are then dealing
with an *abstraction*, not with the concrete fact with which we
are presented in experience. As I have pointed out in
another place, it is all too easy to assume that when we
have dissected this or that object—say, a cat—we have
managed to arrive at the 'essence' of 'cat-ness'. Yet such
is not the case. For we have not been working with a real
and live cat; we have been dissecting a dead cat. And
even in the dissection, something may elude us, since the
chemical changes which follow death do not permit us
to describe 'catness'—what we have been doing, in this
instance, is saying something about how the body of a
dead cat looks and what may be set down as its 'morphology'. The living purring, meowing creature is quite
different. Nor can a cat, to continue with our example,
be understood with any degree of completeness, save in
terms of its relationships. Wherever we turn, we are
confronted by, and we ourselves know that the observer
is, a series of such relationships of greater or less intensity.

In a world like that, we live and move and have our
'becoming' (if one may change a word in the Pauline
text). Now it is the conviction of process thinking that
the chief principle in things, God, is not to be seen as
'the great exception' to what we know so well in the world

and in ourselves. Whitehead's famous aphorism, that God 'is not the exception to all metaphysical principles, invoked to save them from collapse, but their chief exemplification', is to the point here. Notice, however, that Whitehead said 'chief' exemplification. This suggests that while God is indeed like the world in which he is at work and of which (as we have just said) he is the chief creative principle, he is like it in an 'eminent manner'. Furthermore, Whitehead said 'to *all* metaphysical principles', which may suggest to us that in *certain* respects God is different . . . but in what way? I should say that he is different in that he abides in and through all process, he abides in and through it in his identity as creative love, and he is both the principal initiator of all that happens and also the chief recipient of the affects of what happens.

In order to explicate this view, process thinkers have talked—as did Whitehead—of the two 'aspects' of God. In one, which is called 'primordial', he is abstract from the world, eternal, containing 'within himself' all potentialities which might be realised; in the other, which is called 'consequent', he is concrete, everlasting (eminently 'temporal' and not the contradiction of all temporal sequence), and the recipient of all values and the factuality those values 'possess'—not only for his own self-satisfaction or enjoyment, although this is part of the truth, but more particularly for his employment in the continuation of his creative endeavour as the world moves on in its advance from stage to stage. This entails a relationship between God and the world, in which there are influences and affects in both directions.

At this point we arrive at the chief difference between what has been called the 'classical' type of theism and the sort which is accepted by process theology. In the former, God is at worst related only 'logically' to the world and is entirely unaffected by what goes on within it. At best he is believed to be 'love' but his love is so full and complete in itself, like his 'being', that nothing can be added to it and he cannot be affected, in his concrete reality as God, by the world's tragedies or its joys. The theologians who have taken this 'classical' view have sought diligently to find ways in which they can preserve the evangelical stress on God's participation in the world, his love for it, and his knowing most intimately and truly all that goes on in it. But the result has been either an unsatisfactory compromise or a decision, in the last resort, to let the metaphysical conception of 'unmoved mover', or *esse a se subsisten*, or some similar view be the dominant partner.

This can work itself out in various ways. It can be the rationalistic way taken by St. Thomas Aquinas and other scholastics influenced by Aristotle; it can be the voluntaristic one which seems to dominate Calvin's thought— God's *will* is so supreme that nothing can have the slightest effect upon it; or it can be 'morally' stated, as when Bishop Nygren in his famous book *Agape and Eros* refuses to allow to God any of that yearning desire to receive which is associated with the 'erotic' motif and insists that God is only 'self-giving love'. About all these views, including the last, Professor Hartshorne's comment applies: that man is unable to do anything *for* God and hence man's existence is ultimately meaningless in itself, since the only true reality is God. Yet, as Hartshorne rightly notes, the working religion of the believer always seems to include the conviction that 'the service of God' *is* something which is done for him and that it does have its affect in the divine life. By an extension of this principle, Hartshorne adds, we ought to say that whatever happens in the created order, whether it is by man's action or by some other agent, counts profoundly for God.

A conception of God which sees him in mutual relationship with the creation will inevitably go on to say that the evil in the world has its affect upon God, while God is continually at work to reduce or to transform this evil so that it may become an instrument for the accomplishment of the good which he purposes. If that is the case, then the question of evil in the world must be seen from quite a different perspective. God shares in it. He too is concerned to battle against it. His victory is achieved by his overcoming it, but he does this in a fashion which is consistent with his own nature as love and cognizant of the freedom of decision which is present in the realm of creaturely occasions. What is more, God's identification of himself with the world means that he is 'the fellow-sufferer who understands', as Whitehead so finely put it. He can be man's 'strength', since he is the unsurpassable One, who in his love is supremely worshipful, who in his faithfulness and wisdom can 'handle things' and who is able to 'turn man's wrath to his praise'—which we might exegete by saying that he can turn anything which occurs, insofar as it has the slightest redeemable possibility, into an occasion for the good. On the other hand, he can also be our 'refuge', since in association with him we find the Presence that illuminates our own darkness and misery.

Baron von Hügel once wrote to a sorrowing mother that her anguish over the death of her child was 'a drop of God's own love fallen into her heart'. Thus horror at the evil in the natural order, in the animal world, in human suffering, is not a blasphemous refusal to accept 'what God wills'. On the contrary, it is an identification with God in *his* 'horror' over these evils and an alignment of human desire with his desire that such evils be 'handled'. The 'divine compassion' is no pretty phrase but an insight into the very depths of God's own life. It may appear irreverent to state it as I must do, but I shall take the risk: God is doing the very best that he can to 'handle' evil and he both calls and wants his human children to join with him in this enterprise.

But why is there evil in the world? Might it not have been 'made' otherwise? To ask that question is to want a world in which 'the chance to learn love' would be lacking. A long-range creative process, in which things are not ready-made but are coming-to-be, in which also there is genuine and radical freedom which God does not over-turn or reject, must be a world in which the possibility of error, wrong decision, failure to advance, finite refusal to conform to the most widely shared good, is present—and present to such a degree that the possibility becomes a probability, which as we very well know turns into an actuality. The explanation for this is clear enough. We cannot ask why a free agent (of whatever degree of sophistication or self-consciousness) chooses that which is contrary to its own best good and to the best good of others; or if we can, it is only in a proximate sense. The explanation ultimately is that all freedom is self-positing. To know exactly why a free choice is made would be to deny the reality of the free choice. One of the grievous errors of some theologians is to forget this obvious truth.

If freedom is self-positing, we may be led to ask why a world in which such freedom obtains is 'better' than one where good would be achieved automatically. The answer here must be that automatic good is hardly

qualified to be called 'good' at all. If we look deeply
into ourselves we know well enough that when we are
'forced to be good', we feel that we are not agents of
good. Good is accomplished or achieved, not given to us
on a platter. Furthermore, the enjoyment of good presupposes that we have laboured to attain to it—although
in a strange way it still seems to be in the nature of a
'gift'.

What is God 'up to' in this sort of world? Plato's
vision of the *demiourgos* in the *Timaeus* may help us here.

Plato said that the *demiourgos* is himself good and that
being good he wishes to share that good with others.
He is not selfish about it. For Plato the desire to share
goodness explains why there is a world at all. And then
he goes on to say that when conscious agents of good
appeared in the world, they appeared so that they might
reflect or imitate the divine goodness. That was their
purpose; it was to be sharers of good, like their 'creator'.
The world, with all its chanciness and in all its risks, is
the place where this can be made possible. God does not
wish to have things which he can move about and control.
He wants free, conscious, responsive agents, who on their
own behalf seek to express the good which is a reflection
of the boundless divine goodness. To say this is not to
minimise the evil that the world contains; it is only to
say that a world in which evil is possible and probable—
and becomes actual, by free decision—is a better sort of
world than one in which goodness is automatic and hence
not truly goodness at all.

We have noted the social character of the creation.
If occasions for good influence and affect other occasions,
it is clear that a world where free goodness is possible is
also a world where occasions with evil consequences can

and must influence and affect other occasions. God 'handles' the matter, so far as he can do so without overriding the freedom; he also participates in the world, so that he knows, understands, and shares in those evil consequences. But they are there; and they are there as evil. If you wish, they may remain as 'surds', until such time as the ceaseless divine activity has turned them into opportunities for good. There may be some—who knows which and what and how many?—that are irredeemable. These God will prehend, grasp or take into himself, but in a negative fashion, by which the evil will be rejected after all possible good has been extracted and treasured and employed for his purposes.

This is the sort of theodicy (or 'justification of God's way with his world') that process thought would present. To fill out the picture one final consideration must be brought forward. God's consequent nature—that is, God as he concretely 'is' with all the affects and influences that the world has offered and he has accepted—is so superabundant in love that we may speak of the divine 'victory' which brings the divine 'joy'. God is utterly vulnerable; but he is also utterly invulnerable—by this I intend that his love is so indefeasible and so indefatigable, so rich and inexhaustible, that nothing can finally defeat or overcome it or turn it into anything else. To believe that, in the fullest sense, is certainly not easy when we look hard at the evil in the world and in our own experience. But it is the most profound insight of Christian faith that it is so.

What is the origin of that insight? It is in the life of Jesus Christ and above all in his willingness to give himself up to death. Calvary is the heart of the matter. It is no accident that the Cross is the symbol of Christian faith;

it is no accident, either, that the Cross is found on, behind, or above so many of the Church's altars. The Cross is the sign of divine victory over evil by absorbing it and assimilating it and using it. This is why one was always deeply moved by the old reredos in St. Paul's Cathedral in London where Christ was portrayed on the Cross with the words written there: *Sic deus dilexit mundom: This is how God loves the world.*

In the piety of the Catholic and Eastern Orthodox communions, it is customary for the faithful to make over themselves, from time to time, 'the sign of the Cross'. Doubtless this act can become automatic; doubtless some make the sign as if it were some magical charm. But those who have understood what it really means know very well that it signifies an identification of the believer with the self-giving in love which Calvary expresses. That is how we can meet evil. Nor is it an accident that in Christian circles the words Constantine is supposed to have seen (not perhaps in association with Calvary's Cross, in the first instance, but that is irrelevant here) have been taken with complete and devoted seriousness: 'In this sign, you will conquer'.

Our next chapter will be given to a consideration of Calvary and its meaning in Christian faith and in Christian discipleship.

4

Calvary

WE concluded the last chapter by noting that in Christian faith the Cross is absolutely central. It is 'the sign of faith'; and it has become this by no accidental set of circumstances but because of the very nature of the faith itself. As the representation of the Buddha, sunk in contemplation, stands for the religion of millions who follow Gautama's way, so for Christians the Cross is their focal symbol.

Some people have objected to the ancient medieval crosses and the paintings of Jesus crucified. They regard the Grunewald crucifixion as a most horrible thing and they criticise the older practice of using figures of Jesus suffering the agonies of Golgotha. They would prefer, they say, an empty Cross—for after all, is not Jesus risen from the dead, with the victory which Easter Day celebrates? The answer to this is or ought to be quite plain. The triumph of Easter is not some 'happy ending' which reverses all that occurred on that dreadful Good Friday. The triumph of the resurrection of Christ is no denial of the reality of the death which he died. On the contrary, it is the divine vindication of what took place on that day when Jesus hung between two 'thieves' on a hill outside the city of Jerusalem. Failure to recognise this signifies failure to comprehend the true profundity of Christian faith.

Similarly, some people have wished that the representation of Christ on his Cross be by the robing of the figure in the priestly vestments or the royal garb which will manifest visibly the truth that in Christian faith the Victim on Calvary is the Lord of the eucharistic action and the king over the world. Certainly I am far from denying either of these truths—Jesus Christ *is* the lord and host at the Eucharist and he *is* 'crowned with many crowns'. But the eucharistic action by his own word and deed is associated with 'the death which he was to accomplish' and the crown which he wears is a crown of thorns. Once again, then, we are brought back to the stark fact of Calvary; and I cannot do other than regard some of the more 'fashionable' types of representation as highly sentimental and romantic. In an unconscious fashion they too are an evasion of the awful reality of that death.

On the other hand, it would be quite mistaken to separate the Cross from the total life of Jesus Christ. That which happened on the Cross is a placarding before the world of what Jesus was during the whole course of his life among us. He had 'a baptism to be baptised with', as he himself is reported to have said. The baptism was the undergoing of death for what he firmly believed to be the fulfilment of the divine purpose in the world. Naturally he saw this in Jewish terms, inevitably he interpreted it as a Jew must have done. But a medieval saint was not wrong when he said that 'the whole life of Christ is the mystery of the Cross'. Nor are the familiar carols sung at Christmas in error when they so often associate the birth at Bethlehem with the death on Calvary. 'The shadow of the Cross' rests over the whole of the life of Jesus. That life, with its doings and its sayings, can only properly be understood when this is recognised as the case.

And when contemporary theologians say much about

Jesus as 'the Man for others' and speak (as they do) about
his 'contagious freedom', they must not forget that in the
former case he quite literally gave himself 'unto death,
even the death of the Cross' on behalf of those others,
while in the latter the freedom which is 'contagious'
through him was not achieved excepting by the 'sweat and
tears' of suffering and anguish. It is all too easy to be
cheerful about these matters, without facing the stark
facts. The ultimate optimism of Christian faith rests
upon and includes the acceptance of things as they are;
and central to those things is a Man dying.

All this may seem very obvious, at least to those who
have not fallen victim to the sentimentalism and roman-
ticism which I have criticised. Yet it needs to be said
again and again, for the heart of the Christian faith is
here. Far too much is at stake to permit us to slip easily
over the crucifixion. Nor does this suggest that the
Christian disciple is one who is gloomy and hopeless.
He is one who, having faced facts as they are and above
all having faced that central fact, is yet a man of hope who
is enabled to go through life with confidence and in trust.
His ultimate optimism is not at the mercy of the 'changes
and chances of this mortal life', since he has first looked
at reality and has been enabled to possess this ultimate
optimism precisely because the very worst has been seen
for what it is and accepted as it is.

I suppose that many will think that what has so far
been said in this chapter is by way of homiletic exhortation
or devotional meditation. It is nothing of the sort. It is
an attempt to get at what Christian faith, and with it
Christian discipleship, are all about. Thus I feel no need
to apologise for having written as I have done.

The suffering which Jesus was called upon to undergo

was occasioned by 'wicked men', as we say. His death, with its accompanying anguish both mental and physical, was the consequence of that human rejection and condemnation. Hence we cannot say that Jesus was directly the victim of the evil present in the natural world as such, nor of course did he participate in 'animal pain'. But the human suffering which he knew was real enough, although we are not able to measure pain and say (as popular devotional books sometimes do) that his own pain was 'the greatest the world has ever known'. In any event, suffering is not quantitatively measurable in that manner. The death of Jesus was the result of human sin or moral evil. But the fact of dying, with all its painful accompaniments, was none the less a genuine participation in the pain of the world.

It is not that physical suffering, in and of itself, which is the only thing, however. In the gospel stories of the crucifixion, stress is put on the sense of dereliction—certainly in Mark's Gospel. Whether or not Jesus uttered the words, 'My God, my God, why hast thou forsaken me?' the words express this loss of awareness of, perhaps confidence in, the divine presence. They are a stark statement of the way in which evil, of whatever sort, can call in question the love of God, his care for his world, and his unfailing availability to his human children. This Jesus himself knew. And that is part of the main significance of Calvary. But we must speak about this at greater length.

We have already noted the horror which all of us feel in the presence of evil. Whether this is natural evil, animal suffering, or human pain—or any variations on these—the terrible consequence of our contemplating evil is the sense that it serves no immediate and obvious purpose: it appears to be unnecessary. A man or woman who does not share this horror at evil is so insensitive that most of us would regard him as less than truly human. Furthermore, the fact of evil, so seen, brings to us the doubt that a genuinely good and loving God can exist when so much also exists which calls into question that love and goodness. This is a feeling that is deeper than sentimentality—it is a soul-shaking feeling. If God is truly good and loving, known to be such on quite other grounds, how can he have 'deserted' his world? There is the sting.

For one who has no such prior belief in God, the existence of evil in the world cannot constitute anything like so serious a problem. The atheist, for example, may be horrified by evil; if he is a truly human being he will be horrified. But for him evil cannot be a problem in the sense in which it is a problem for one who has been brought to believe that the chief casual principle in the world is good. The non-believer cannot avoid the presence of evil. He like everyone else must learn how to handle it. But the question which faces him is not the question of 'Why?' It is the question of 'How?'

As a matter of fact, that last is also the question which the believer must ask himself. It may be the only question which the believer can come anywhere near really answering. But for him the prior question is also posed in the most serious and terrifying manner: 'Why is there this evil?' We have already said that it cannot be answered in any completeness. We have spoken of the ameliorating considerations which may be adduced, but have insisted that they do not remove the fact of evil. We have also said that the nearest we can get to an answer to the question 'Why?' will be found by the introduction of such conceptions as the last chapter was concerned to present: the sort of world this is, the sort of God about whom one may reasonably (and faithfully) speak, the sort of purpose which that God has in view, the limitations which are imposed upon God as well as upon the world, and finally what may rightly be said about the use that such a God can make of the evil which is present. Beyond that, surely, we cannot go; we remain finite intelligences and we do not have the material upon which those intelligences might work to provide an adequate, much less a complete, answer.

But what the Cross brings to us is the assurance that in 'all their afflictions' God was and is 'afflicted'. This identification of God with his world, not by becoming that world but by being utterly participant in it, is spoken out to us, placarded before us, made plain to us, on Calvary. To say this, however, is also to say something about who Jesus was and is. If he were nothing more than 'another man', called upon to suffer pain and endure death, there would be no specifically Christian insight. In that case, we should only have one more instance of the horror of evil. The problem would be aggravated; it would not be illuminated. Yet Christian faith sees in Jesus more than 'another man'. That he *is* man, in the fullest sense, is asserted; it is also claimed that there is more here than meets the observer unless that observer has 'the eye of faith'. If he does have such faith, the something more is the most startling and most encouraging fact in the history of the human race.

Earlier in this book I have urged what I styled 'the organic nature' of Christian faith. Other theologians have emphasised the same point. Nowhere is that organic nature more plainly seen than in connection with the subject we are here discussing. We must turn, therefore, to the doctrine of the person of Christ.

That doctrine has commonly been regarded as distinct from the doctrine of the work of Christ. In most textbooks of Christian theology, the chapter which deals with 'who Christ is' precedes that on 'what Christ does'. But surely this order of things is wrong, since it is only in terms of what Christ did and does that we have any reason to be interested in 'who he is'. There is a further point, however. Increasingly theologians find that is is impossible to think about Christ's 'person' as in any way distinct from his 'work'. Some of them, at least, would say that the basic concern is best expressed in such language as 'what God did in Christ'. This suggests an even more radical application of the famous saying of Melancthon, that 'to know Christ is to know, not his natures, but his benefits'.

Those theologians who have been affected by the conceptuality offered in process thought, as well as others who have approached the matter from some other conceptuality, are disinclined to employ the traditional christological terms about 'natures' and 'person'. As everybody knows, the classically formulated doctrine about Jesus is that in him we have 'one person with two natures'. One nature is human, 'of the substance of the Virgin Mary his Mother'; the other is divine, 'of the substance of God the Father'. The 'person' of the union of these natures is commonly regarded as divine; this is the person of the Eternal Word of God, who is said to have 'assumed human nature' but not a human 'person'. Had he done the latter, there would have been two persons in the incarnate Lord which for thinkers in the period of patristic christology would have been an intolerable idea.

One of the most powerful recent criticisms of all this
doctrinal interpretation is the essay in *Soundings* by Canon
Hugh Montefiore; but he is not alone in his rejection.
I may immodestly note that I myself have written in a
similar vein in two books (*The Word Incarnate* and
Christology Reconsidered); and a very careful and thorough
critique forms part of the late Donald Baillie's *God was
in Christ*. Neither Montefiore nor Baillie accepts the
process conceptuality, yet their critique is as devastating
as my own, which *was* written from this point-of-view.
All of us—and we do not stand alone here—believe that
the static categories of 'nature' and 'person', in the sense
in which the patristic age used them and in which some
contemporary 'orthodox' theologians (like E. L. Mascall)
would still defend them, can no longer serve us. They are
a barrier to interpretation of Christ, rather than an aid
for that interpretation. All of us would wish to put in
their place a dynamic view, in which 'act' rather than
'substance' is central, and in which the meaning given
to 'person' is the modern one which is used in every area
of discussion (save that of 'orthodox' theology) rather
than an inert conception of 'person' as 'an individual
substance of a rational nature', as St. Thomas, following
Boethius, defined the term.

Nor is it only theologians who have taken this line.
Professor John Knox, among distinguished contemporary
New Testament scholars, has argued in a series of important books that an 'act-christology' is much more in
accord with the general biblical (and especially the New
Testament) outlook. He speaks of 'the act of God' which
was accomplished in and through the 'event of Jesus
Christ', an 'event' which he interprets in a very interesting
fashion as including the whole complex of antecedent

preparation, concomitant reception, and future consequences, all of these finding their focus in the Man of Nazareth—a way of seeing the matter which naturally commends itself to any process thinker, since it is both a dynamic and a societal interpretation of 'event'.

I have written the preceding paragraphs as a preparation for my insistence that in the total organic reality of Christian faith, Jesus Christ is taken to be that point in which God is most importantly active, so far as human experience and human history are concerned. God has indeed been active and he continues to be active elsewhere; his activity will be as much a part of the future as it has been of the past and is of the present. Yet, because of what he effects in the lives of those who in faith commit themselves to Christ and his Spirit of participatory love, he is the central figure in this whole movement. This is of faith; it cannot be demonstrated. Nor would any modern Christian wish to adopt an imperialistic attitude in such matters in respect to other religious faiths. These are to be regarded with reverence and accepted as ways in which God, through his activity, has also disclosed himself to his human children. But the stance of specifically Christian faith is that in this Jesus, whatever else may be true elsewhere, God is at work; and that in a manner unprecedented in degree of fulness, adequate to our human situation, and in a decisive manner revelatory of what God is and of what God is 'up to' in the world. Jesus cannot be viewed as the supreme anomaly, for that would deny his truly revelatory significance; he must be viewed, by those who have been touched by his Spirit, as the classical instance of God's working in the creation. This is my own phrasing, already used in several other pieces of writing; but I repeat it

confidently, since in my judgement it provides a useful
distinction between mistaken ways of envisaging Jesus'
importance and what I take to be the sound (and deeply
Christian) way of envisaging it.

For our present subject, the conclusion which may be
drawn is very clear. In the life of the Man of Nazareth,
all of it 'under the shadow of the Cross', and supremely
in the events of the last few days culminating in the passion
and death on Calvary, *God* is involved. This human action
of the Man Jesus is at the same moment a reflection—even
more, a genuine participation—of the divine causal and
affective principle we call God. Hence if we wish to know
'what God is like', how he works in the world, what his
manner and mode of operation truly is, the place to
look is there—in the seamless robe of that life and death.
That is how God is, that is how God works, that is how
God takes to himself what happens in the world.

I have said that this is of faith, not to be demonstrated.
Yet I should add that once it has been accepted as true,
tremendous light is thrown on the question of evil in the
world. Every thinking person is obliged to adopt some
stance towards life, as the existentialists have so insistently
argued; even those who in theory refuse to adopt a
stance cannot avoid doing so, although in their case it is
a stance of detachment which renders them less than
authentic human persons. A friend once said that if one
must adopt a stance, one could certainly choose no stance
more enabling and ennobling, more courageous yet more
demanding, than the stance of Christian faith as it has just
been defined. To believe that in Jesus God's 'nature and
his agency in the world' (in Whitehead's fine phrase) is
'disclosed in act', is to take a risk. That cannot be
denied. But it is also to find strength for living in the face

of the evil which confronts us and which we cannot evade
or seek to minimise.

The points just made might be summed up in this way.
In the Man Jesus we are enabled to see that God identifies
himself with his world, that he bears the suffering which
men must know in that world, and that in knowing this
suffering he shares also in that kind of dereliction which
the cry on the Cross so poignantly symbolises. Richard
Baxter's familiar hymn says of Christ, 'He leads us through
no darker rooms/Than he's been through before . . .'
If what we have been arguing is true of Christian faith,
Baxter's words apply not only to Christ, as the Man
of Nazareth, but also to God. For in the theologically
inadequate yet existentially moving language of an ancient
Christian hymn-writer, '*God* is reigning from a Tree'.
The only crown he wears is a crown of thorns; the only
throne he occupies is a Cross; the only rule he exercises
is the reign of suffering and participant love.

We have not finished the story, however. It will be
recalled that in beginning this chapter, something was
said about the relationship of Good Friday and Easter
Day as they are reported to us in the gospels. The story
is told us, all the way through, as a paradoxical combina-
tion of Victim and Victor—the one who suffers is the one
who triumphs. The story comes 'with the note of authentic
victory', as Whitehead once said. Precisely; and such
references as those about God's reigning 'from the Tree'
confirm this.

'Easter triumph, Easter joy' are not the conventional
happy-ending, then. They are the vindication of what
was done in Christ's life and in his suffering and death.
It is as if God had written over Calvary, 'That is how I
myself really am. That is how I am related to the world's

pain in the face of evil. That is what I do about it.' But of course God would do nothing like that; it is his way to be self-veiled rather blatantly than to announce his presence among us. Dietrich Bonhoeffer has much to teach us on this point, if we will only listen—God lets himself be edged out of the world, lets himself be affected by the world's evil and pain, and lets us be in similar case. Yet in such a world, which seems to be 'without' or 'apart from' God, men are enabled to live 'before God' and 'with God'.

For altogether too long Christian theology has been enamoured of earthly majesty, sheer dictatorial power, and unyielding moralistic condemnation—taking these as fitting to apply to the divine character. The consequence of this attitude is easy to see. Oriental majesty, suitable for the court of some sultan, dictatorial control of the citizenry, intolerable and impossible demands made upon the subjects—all this has been expressed in liturgy and in theological teaching. About all this Whitehead, whom we have quoted so frequently (and I hope, so aptly), commented that in at least certain quarters the Church appears to have 'given to God that which belongs exclusively to Caesar'. I think that he was correct in saying this. He did not draw the corollary—that because of this misapplication of ideas, the evil which is so much a factor of our experience is made even more appalling. For if God is in fact a sultan or dictator, with the trappings and apparatus appropriate to such a status, he is lowered in his moral character—an all-powerful deity, directly responsible for what happened in the world and entirely capable of coping with it, who failed to do just this coping, would not be as good as a good man. He would be a monster. Alas, the portrayal of God in some Christian teaching makes him very much this sort of monster.

On the other hand, if God is indeed the chief causative principle, but not the only one; if there is a radical freedom in the creation by virtue of which decisions may be made, at whatever level of consciousness or self-awareness, which are either for or against the best good; and if God is also the 'supreme affect' (in Schubert Ogden's splendid phrase), so that he is participant in, identified with, and recipient from the creation—then things are very different indeed.

It may be argued by a critic that such a God is finite, perhaps even impotent. What reason have we to think that his purpose of good will in the long run show itself victorious over the evil in the natural world, the suffering in the animal creation and in human life, the anguish known in human experience—and also the wrong-choosing, wrong-thinking, and wrong-doing of men?

In truth, however, God so conceived is not finite in any pejorative meaning of that word. He is simply love; and being love, he acts lovingly. He does not coerce, he does not force, he does not negate freedom. These are not in his nature. He acts in the world by the lure and invitation and solicitation about which we have already spoken. He is confronted by material with which he must work. But since he is the giver of all 'initial aims' which are to be brought to actualisation as the accepted 'subjective aim' of each creature, he is not confronted with something that is utterly alien to him and with which he must deal as if it were quite impatient of his action within it and through it. It is his world, in the sense that he is always making and re-making it. We do not know anything about some supposed pre-creational state when God 'existed' alone—in fact, to talk in this way is to suppose that a creator once upon a time did not create, which would seem absurd. His creativity is an everlasting activity, presupposing something creatively done and the results of that creative doing in a world which is not identical with God but which yet is 'his' world.

Very well, it may be said, but what about 'final' victory? I hope that the answer proper to that question has already been indicated. Calvary, seen in the light of Easter, is a window into the heart of God himself. In him the pain and suffering, the evil in the world, whatever and wherever it may be, has been received so far as it possesses any redeemable possibilities. If there is anything left over which is totally irredeemable, only God knows what it is—certainly we do not. But if there is, it is left behind in the past which is now dead and over with, although its influence is still known in the present— and in God, too, since he has experienced it. What has taken place in the creation, in its various occasions, has made a difference to God and in God.

It has made a difference to him, for it has presented him with that with which he deals. He has cared for the world always; now he cares for it in this or that particular patterning or configuration. And he deals with it as it is, to secure from its employment all that may be drawn from it for the furthering of the ends of love. It has made a difference in him, too, for it has either enriched and enhanced the divine joy—'there is joy in heaven', let us remember, and joy can be augmented—or it has brought to his heart of love an anguish which is beyond anything that we know. Our own anguish is a share in his—not something alien to the divine life.

But—and finally—since in the paradigm case of Calvary (the 'classic instance of what God is and is "up to" in his world') we who are faithful have been granted the deepest possible insight into what God is like and what he is accomplishing, we have also the assurance of faith that evil can be made into an occasion of good, so that nothing worthy of saving is lost. In the divine wisdom it is seen for what it is, used as it is, and open to transformation. Evil is not to be done so that good may abound; it is blasphemous and a further denial of God's nature of love when men speak in that fashion. But once evil has happened, it can be used. In thus using it and conquering over it, God manifests himself as the indefeasible and indefatigable love that he is.

If this be the case, then those who know him for what he is have their own response to make. It is with that response that we shall concern ourselves in the following chapter.

5

Our Response

EVIL is in the world as an accompaniment of a processive advance in which good is being achieved through a continuing forward movement. The world in which this evil—natural disaster, animal suffering, the anguish known in human experience—is present is not remote from its chief causative source which men call God; he is transcendent, but in no sense which would suggest that he is not involved in and participant with the world. He identifies himself with the world, he works ceaselessly in the world in the mode appropriate to his nature as love, and from the world he elicits the free response which will contribute to the ongoing production of genuine good.

Furthermore, in the two-way relationship between God and the creation, there is a certain give-and-take on both sides. What God is and does affects the creation; what the creation, with its capacity for decision, is and does affects God. He is himself unsurpassable by anything which is not himself; yet in his own consequent nature, which is deity in concrete manifestation and in concrete existence, he is open to new 'experiences' and to the enhancement which they may bring. But precisely because of his relationship with the creation, he receives into himself what happens in the creation, sharing in its sorrow and rejoicing in its joy which he also shares. He is superabundant love, completely inexhaustible and able to adjust himself to what occurs, able also to adjust what

occurs to his own purpose of further good. He makes
this adjustment, however, through and not against the
freedom which is radical in creation; hence it is all a
matter of lure and enticement, of persuasion rather than
of coercion. Love is the key or clue to his activity, as it is
also the key or clue to his own nature.

This is a brief summary of our argument in two earlier
of the preceding chapters. But it must be remembered
that in the last chapter the stress was on Calvary as the
symbol and effective sign of God's very heart. There men
have been given the opportunity to see deep into God.
He is demonstrated, for those who have the 'eyes of faith',
as the One who is so deeply participant, so intimately
identified, with the creation, that its evil is known to him
with an intensity which no created thing could know.
At the same time, he 'deals with evil' with a wisdom which
no created thing could possess. And in thus dealing
with it, he triumphs over it. He is not defeated by evil,
for Christian faith sees that in the event of Jesus Christ
Good Friday and Easter Day are so linked that the evil
which in this case was done *by* men became an occasion
for the greatest good which could be accomplished *for*
men. The account of the life of Christ, focussed in his
self-giving to the point of death, is told 'with the note of
authentic victory', since those who were with Jesus as
his disciples were convinced that the Victim was the Victor.

If this had been but another instance of human existence
and nothing else, the conviction in all its splendour and
with all its poignancy could not have been entertained.
But Christian faith, beginning with the undeveloped
loyalty, love, and worship of the disciples before the last
days of Jesus' life and more and more penetrating into the
meaning of that life, discerned that here was an activity

of God which was of the highest importance—so much so that they could not interpret their Master and Lord in terms which were less than those applicable to God himself. First through Jewish thought-forms, then with the use of concepts derived from the hellenistic world of the time, and finally in precise words which in their time were the only ones available to state this conviction, they said that God was here. He was here in a Man, of course; they could not deny for a moment the reality of that humanity which the first disciples had known. But in some fashion, in and through and by and with that humanity in its genuine human fullness, there was the activity of God.

Contemporary Christian believers may not find the terminology of the Patristic age suitable for us today. Increasingly modern theologians have recognised this and have sought for language which will be appropriate for our times. But the same *conviction* is basic throughout the development of Christian thought. There have been mistakes. Sometimes the divinity present and at work in the Man Jesus has been emphasised in such a way that there was peril to his humanity. Sometimes, as in certain modern writers, the humanity has been stressed so that the truth of the divine activity has been obscured. Often, the way in which the coincidence of that activity and true humanity has been envisaged has been artificial. And we can have no doubt that for most of Christian history the so-called 'uniqueness' of Jesus has been stated in a manner which made him appear an alien invader of a world which otherwise and elsewhere was without the divine presence and untouched by the divine activity. None the less, we owe it to our fathers in the faith to see that they did the very best they could, under the particular conditions which were theirs and with the use of language which was natural to their minds, to maintain the conviction. We may think that we have better terms to use in working out a christology; doubtless we do. Future ages, however, may find the pattern, which to us is right, to be one that makes little or no appeal to them. Then they too will have to re-conceive, in whatever idiom is available to them, the affirmation that 'God was in Christ' and that in Christ he disclosed his heart and effectively acted to make new and authentic existence possible for his children—not by selecting a few who would be 'saved' but by 're-presenting' (as Schubert Ogden has well put it) in this particular and focal instance, what God is always 'up to' with respect to his human children.

The insight of this faith in God as the suffering lover who understands and accepts and conquers sin is to be extended, we have urged, to our consideration of evil in its more general sense. But, we asked, what sort of response does this expect from the human side?

Christian piety has spoken with St. Paul of the obligation upon disciples 'to make up what is lacking in the sufferings of Christ, for his Body's sake, which is the Church'. That is one way of putting the response. Another, familiar to us from the popular hymns of the Church, tells the disciple that he must himself 'bear the Cross'. A gospel hymn affirms (to repeat Dr. Brown's quotation) that 'There's a cross for everyone/And there's a cross for me'. More pedantically, the response which the placarding of Christ on his cross, before the eyes of those who know and love him, demands from us and evokes from us is the making real in our own lives that spirit of self-identification with the world's pain which was God's act in Christ.

Now to talk like this entails first of all a realistic appraisal of evil as it is. We have mentioned this when we discussed the fact of evil in its various manifestations. At that point we insisted that no Christian can shut his eyes to evil, pretend that it is not there, try to explain it in such a fashion that he succeeds in 'explaining it away'. In the long run and in the last resort, there may be some truth—how much is a nice question—in the line of Pope, 'partial evil, universal good'; but as it stands it is absurd and unintelligible to anyone who has himself felt evil or has entered into the experience of others who are feeling it with its horrible intensity. The cults which attempt to get away from the facts are only for sentimentalists or for those who are content to look the other way when evil appears.

Once evil has been faced, it must also be felt—or so I understand the proper Christian response. By this I mean to suggest that it must become the occasion for the sympathetic awareness or sensitivity in which each of us knows what evil is and is outraged by its existence. If the evil happens to oneself, above all, it must not be made an occasion for self-pity: Yet at the same time the 'soul is encouraged to cry itself out', as Baron von Hügel phrased it. The Epicurean may attempt to avoid any participation in suffering; the Stoic may endure it in cold contempt. But the Christian is different. He need not be in the least ashamed of the horror he feels, nor need he 'keep back the tears', for himself or for others. There is all the difference in the world between sentimental self-pity and this sort of readiness to express one's deepest feelings.

It is difficult for Anglo-Saxons, especially those of my own older generation, to take this point. We have been brought up from childhood to think that any expression of feeling is unmanly; the 'stiff-upper lip' attitude to life has been drilled into us to such a degree that we are quite literally afraid to let ourselves see, or anyone else see, the depth of our 'feeling-tones'. I have a suspicion that a good deal of nervous and emotional breakdown is due to this inhuman training. Had we been able from time to time to express our sense of horror, our depth of pain, our personal anguish (especially for what happens to other people), we should not be so likely to collapse when the final straw has been laid on our backs—if this mixed metaphor will be acceptable! In those lands where the expression of emotion is taken as a normal and natural matter, the attitude is I think much healthier. Somebody remarked that the Latin peoples are not so likely to become emotionally disordered, in any severe sense, since they have all along been able to find an outlet for their feelings and have not been ashamed of the expression of them.

I have mentioned Baron von Hügel's splendid urging that we 'cry ourselves out'. But that is not all he said in his essay on suffering. He also said that a Christian is one who in his response to the exigencies of life knows how to 'grasp life's nettle boldly'. This is the other side of the feeling of and for evil. What is at stake here is a courageous attitude in the face of obstacles. It is the spirit which grapples honestly and openly with what is wrong in the world and refuses to be 'laid low' by what happens. That too is how a disciple of Jesus will act when he has first accepted and then felt evil for what it is.

He must also try to do something about it.

I know of no more eloquent discussion of this than may be found scattered through the writings of Professor

Leonard Hodgson. In his case, the reference is especially to the Church and its failure to see that it is *not* intended to provide a refuge from trouble but is rather an army concerned to 'rescue the world' from whatever is evil in it. As he notes, far too often theologians have portrayed the Church as 'the ark of salvation', in which the 'elect' are enabled to get through this life towards their heavenly destiny. But he insists that this is treason to the spirit of Jesus Christ. The only way a man can be saved, Hodgson says, is by himself becoming a saviour—one who in the Spirit of and by the power released in Jesus works for the bringing of love, justice, understanding, and everything good to more people in more places. Thus he fights evil, knowing that because it is an outrage to God (as we have seen), it is also an outrage to every good man.

That 'drop of God's love' in human hearts which manifests true acceptance of facts, horror at what is evil in them, and deep participation in the world's suffering, leads to action. If it does not do so, it can also be nothing more than sentimentality. In any event, Christian discipleship is in 'doing the truth', as the Fourth Gospel makes clear to us; and a Christian who is not led to act for the removal of evil demonstrates that he has not fully been grasped by his professed discipleship.

This labour, 'overcoming evil with good', may be carried out in most diverse ways. Very few of them are specifically 'religious'. The engineer who is led to work for the control of river-floods is performing exactly this service; so is the doctor or nurse in a hospital ward. Wherever human beings are caught up in this effort to replace what is wrong with what is right, what is ugly with what is beautiful, what is false with what is true, what is hateful with what is loving, what is a matter of prejudice with attempts at understanding, what is unfair and unjust with social righteousness—need the list be continued?—they are making the response which is peculiarly theirs. They are 'making up for their part' what was incomplete in the full application and implementation of Christ's participation in the world for good. And they are manifesting in their actions the loving concern which is God's very heart. In other words, most of our response to the fact of evil, when we look at it as God has enabled us to do and in his spirit, is likely to be in 'secular' channels and through 'secular' agencies.

Reinhold Niebuhr is said to be the author of a prayer which has frequently been used by those working for social justice. The prayer speaks of our 'having the courage for changing what can be changed' and the patience for 'accepting what cannot be changed'; and it asks for the wisdom to 'know the difference between them'. This prayer may be applied to our own topic. There are some evils about which we can do little or nothing, such as the earthquakes and tidal waves to which we have referred—all we can do is to accept them as they come, feel the difficulty they present and the possible damage to life and limb that they may bring, and (in whatever way possible) seek to arrange the affairs of men so that they will not be exposed to such dangers. But there are many evils about which we can do something. We can refuse to inflict needless pain in the animal world; we can care for the sick and labour to find cures for their illnesses; we can comfort the dying and the bereaved. We can also do something about those social injustices which are, to be sure, the long-range result of man's wrong moral decisions but for which nobody may be immediately responsible. Certainly we need to know what we can do and how, what we cannot do and why.

All this is part of the specific Christian vocation; but it is also a duty laid upon all men of good-will. The difference between such men and the Christian is that the latter knows, or believes he knows, that he is labouring for and with God in the handling of evil. He has the image of Christ before him. He has the courage, at the least the possibility of securing the courage, of continuing when the going gets very hard. He can thus be saved from 'faithless fears and worldly anxieties', as the American Prayer Book phrases it; and he can be delivered from that sense of futility which is so likely to surge up in any man when he is faced with the almost insuperable obstacles which evil in all its forms presents to him.

To see evil for what it is: to feel the anguish of it and its results: to act vigorously, to the limit of our capacity, for its overcoming—such is the response which the Christian makes, once he has known the real 'glory of God in the face of Jesus Christ'. There is another aspect of his response, however; and this is peculiarly difficult to state, since almost inevitably one may appear to suggest quite mistaken and quite unchristian ideas. The matter was summed up by John Keats when he wrote that while he could not see the world as a 'vale of tears', he could see it as a 'vale of soul-making'.

Of course an informed Christian cannot accept any notion of a dualism between 'soul' and 'body'. It is the whole personality which must be taken into account. Hence we ought not to talk about 'soul-making'; we should talk about the making of a human personality. Human personality is brought into actuality as the given

of the past is used in the context of present relationships
to establish the realisation ('the making real', in the
fullest sense) of the aim or purpose or 'vocation' of each
human occasion or series (or routes) of occasions. Human
life is a process in each of us—it is indeed a 'making'.
But we must be careful lest we speak as if it were merely
towards some 'heavenly home' where the woes of this
world will be forgotten. Any such simply futuristic idea
of fulfilment, in which we put into the 'next world' what
ought to be accomplished in this one, is a fraudulent
version of what the Christian hope is really about.

Yet there is something important in Keat's comment.
It *is* true that the facing of evil, the handling of it, and the
overcoming of it in the Spirit (and by the power) of Jesus
Christ, can bring about an enrichment of human personality. The man or woman who has had a too easy life,
with no obstacles to overcome, no struggles to face, no
pain to bear, no sympathy to show, is a sorry specimen of
manhood. On the other hand, we should not think that
we can talk glibly about this kind of development of
human character. There are many men and women who
have been embittered and hardened, sometimes through
no fault of their own, by what has happened to them.
Suffering does not always ennoble; endurance of evil
does not always bring about 'sweeter' men and women.
There has been a good deal of romantic devotional
nonsense about this. And yet, and yet . . . As I have
said, there *is* something important here.

I think that nowhere is it better phrased than in a
passage in Soren Kierkegaard's *Journals*. Let me quote
the passage in full; it is on page 467 (and following) in
Alexander Dru's translation:

'As a skilful cook says of a dish in which there are

already a great many ingredients: "It still needs just a little pinch of cinnamon" (and we perhaps could hardly tell by the taste that this little pinch had been added, but she knew precisely why and precisely how it affected the taste of the whole mixture); as an artist says with a view to the colour effect of a whole painting which is composed of many, many colours: "There and there, at that little point, it needs a little touch of red" (and we perhaps could hardly even discover the red, so carefully has the artist shaded it, although he knows exactly why it should be introduced). So it is with providence. O, the providence of the world is a vast housekeeping, a grandiose painting. Yet he, the Master, God in Heaven, behaves like the cook and the artist. He says: "There must be a little pinch of spice here, a little touch of red." We do not understand why, we are hardly aware of it, since that little bit is so thoroughly absorbed in the whole. But God knows why. A little pinch of spice! That is to say: Here a man must be sacrificed, he is needed to impart a particular taste to the rest. These are the correctives. It is a woeful error for the one who is used to apply the corrective to become impatient and try to make the corrective the norm. That is an attempt to bring everything to confusion. A little pinch of spice! Humanly speaking, what a painful thing, thus to be sacrificed, to be the little pinch of spice. But on the other hand, God knows well the man he elects to use in this way, and then he knows also, in an inward understanding of it, how to make it a blessed thing for him to be sacrificed, that among the thousands of divers voices which express, each in its own way, the same thing, his will also be heard, and perhaps especially his, which is truly *de profundis*, proclaiming: God is love. The birds on the branches, the lilies in the field, the deer in the forest, the fish in the sea, countless hosts of happy men exultantly proclaim: God is love. But beneath all these sopranos, supporting them as it were like the bass part, is audible the *de profundis* which issues from those who are sacrificed: God is love.'

The only criticism I should wish to make of this splendid passage is that it seems to suggest that God, as 'the providence of the world', is himself the directly responsible agent for each and every 'pinch of spice'. In our third chapter we discussed this mistaken notion and substituted for it a world of inter-relationships (a 'societal' world) in which no such final responsibility is to be ascribed to God. The reason for this, it will be recalled, was the radical freedom in the creation. Hence it is wrong to 'blame God' for everything that happens; he is one of the causes, the chief one indeed, but by no means the only one. Kierkegaard's related notion of the 'elect man' needs modification too.

Granted this, however, Kierkegaard has beautifully made his main point. It has to do with what we do with the evil we must face. This is the last thing to be said about the Christian response to evil. What do we do about it, so far as we ourselves are concerned? His answer is that we find in it a way of offering our own lives for the good which is God; and that, being 'sacrificed' after the model of our Lord and our Pattern Jesus Christ, we also proclaim the great Christian faith that 'God is love'.

When I was young, it was customary for teachers of Christian spirituality to speak much about 'offering our suffering to God'. The theology implied by much that they said was, I am sure, quite inadequate. But the main thrust of their teaching was by no means entirely wrong.

When there is nothing else we can do about some instance of evil, we can identify ourselves with God in his ways of handling it—we can 'take' things, as the American slang phrase puts it, and in our personal lives as well as in the worship of the Christian fellowship relate them to God, opening ourselves to be used by him in whatever ways may be right and possible, so that his will may more perfectly be done in the world—and done through us and the offering of ourselves. This is no running away from evil, no minimising of its horrible aspect, and no refusal to do whatever we can about it. On the contrary, this is a plain recognition of our finite and limited perspective and our readiness to offer ourselves to the divine wisdom 'which sweetly orders all things', working in all things for their ordering towards good.

The theological implications of this participation of the human response to evil in the divine response to it ought to be plain enough. Perhaps at this point, more clearly than at any other, the inadequacy of a concept of God as essentially self-contained, with sheer *aseity* as his root-attribute, is demonstrated. That concept is philosophically inadequate, I should argue; but even more important for the Christian, it is untrue to the real facts of genuine worship and devotion. The religious person never considers God as remote and uninterested; if he did he could not adore him, pray to him, wish to serve him, and offer himself to him in this way. He could only cringe before him in servile submission. To speak of worship is to speak of a two-way relationship, in which something is done by and something is done for each of the parties. And we worship only that which is worshipful—that is, worthy of the stance of worship directed towards him. Ultimately, this is God as love, God as supreme excellence,

God as sheer perfection in the goodness of his concern for the creation.

Thus it is no accident that when the Christian discerns in Jesus Christ the signal instance of God's activity in the world—and in consequence, the signal disclosure of God's nature—he is impelled to respond. His response is the human reflection of God's own heart and God's own way. If God handles the evil in the world in the manner which Calvary reveals, the response is by identification with the divine handling. So, to sum it up, the Christian response is an honest recognition of evil for what it is, a profound sense of outrage at its consequences, a dedication to the removal of such evil as can be removed, and throughout the enterprise an offering of self to the purposes of love. Thus the Christian, one hopes in an especially clear way, but also every other man or woman who is moving towards authenticity of life, can come to live 'in love'—which is to say, he is enabled to live 'in God', whose love for his world is 're-presented' (once again to use Schubert Ogden's telling verb) in the Man Jesus. In that sense and that way, he can make his own the cry of St. Paul, 'Thanks be to God, who giveth us the victory through Jesus Christ our Lord'.

6

The Conclusion of the Matter

SEVERAL years ago, I received a letter from a young woman whom I did not know but who had heard of my name as the author of books on Christian faith. This young woman lived in the western part of the United States. She was in her mid-twenties. She wrote that she had been a student, hoping for a future in which she might be of some service to her fellow-men. Then, she told me, she had been stricken with the ghastly illness called multiple sclerosis. For seven years she had been suffering from this ailment; doctors seemed to think that her condition was a continuingly serious one. She was a Christian believer and when active had been regular in church attendance; even now, bed-ridden much of the time, she 'said her prayers' and tried to maintain her Christian faith. But the problem of evil, in the form of suffering such as she experienced, was for her a terrible one. How, she asked, could the loving God in whom she had faith permit such a thing? Would I write her a letter, short or long, which might be of help to her as she tried to face her pain and live with it as a given fact, yet without doubting the love of God and his care for his human children?

I wrote her a long letter; and because I thought that from time to time there might be other people who were in her situation and might turn to me for help, I kept a copy of that letter. In one form or another it has given some slight assistance to other correspondents. And I venture to end this part with a reproduction of what I wrote, since the letter sums up much of what has been said in its several chapters and may serve as a kind of 'pastoral' application of the position which I have been urging upon the reader.

'You ask me, why do people suffer? And I know that you ask it with all the more urgency because you yourself have been the victim, for seven years now, of a painful and apparently incurable disease.

'It is a very hard question, not only because the problem which it poses is itself a difficult one, but also because any answer which might be given is in danger of seeming to claim more knowledge than any human being could ever claim to possess. But there are some things that I can say. I say them in all humility, yet with the confidence which springs from my own conviction that in the big things of life the Christian faith which you and I share gives us the best insight into the meaning of human life and the world where we live as men.

'The first thing that I would say is that this world in which we live is not a world that is a finished product— complete and final as it stands. It is a world which is still being made, a world where things are on the move towards their completion. And the God in whom we believe is the creator of the world; but his creation is a long continuing, perhaps never-ceasing, process. He does this creating in a subtle way, giving everything its aim or purpose and then urging it on by loving lure to the fulfilment of that purpose. He is not like a carpenter, working on things; he is like an artist, eliciting from the stuff with which he works its own potential beauty and harmony and loveliness. He is also the sovereign ruler of the world, but not as a manipulator; he rules through his love—which after all is the only kind of rule which in the long run can secure the consent and cooperation of his creation.

'So creation is not something that has happened and is now done. It is something that began in the past, if it did not always go on; and it is something that does not stop. The poet Alfred Noyes once wrote these lines: 'Now and forever/God makes earth and heaven.' That puts it very well, I think. It is wrong to take any given particular moment and say, "*There*: it's done. Creation is now finished and we have to give some account of what it's all about exactly as it is." That would be a very short-range view. Rather, we should see that something is being made by God, in his own loving and concerned way. He has designs which he is working out, patiently, tirelessly, and (yes, I dare to say it) painfully. What he is up to can be understood only through what is "coming to be", by the goals in view, not by things as they happen to be at this or that time.

'In a world like that, with God working in it in that way, we see a process of evolutionary development. This means that God is active as he makes things make themselves. In this way he takes account of the real freedom that created things, including you and me as human persons, possess as one of their chief characteristics. He uses that freedom which is ours and the world's; but he uses it so that we are "co-workers together with him". He does not pull us about, as if we were marionettes on a string. He respects our freedom and wants us to make our own contribution to the whole vast enterprise.

'Since we are people like that, in a world which is like that, there has to be a real chance that things will go wrong. If there were not that chance, there would be no freedom—and freedom means decisions which may be made for good or for ill. And the ways in which things may go wrong are innumerable. Some of them are the result of our own foolishness. Often they come about because we wish to have our own way without any regard for bigger and better goals. And a great many of them, I think, are just there as part of what it means to be a world "in process of becoming". You might say—I would—that a certain chanciness is inevitable in a world like that.

'This "going wrong" about which I have written is called "evil". The part of it which is due to narrowly self-centred choices of men has been named "sin" by religiously-minded people. All of it is contrary to God's plan and interferes with the fulfilment of that aim. Yet God remains the sovereign ruler who is able to work to bring things to himself, so that his aim or plan does get accomplished, even if that is done with difficulty and with pain to himself. Much of this "redeeming" is done very subtly and is quite invisible to our eyes. It is a keeping of things within a broad pattern so that they are not entirely out of control. Some of the "redeeming" is known to us through what we call "the eyes of faith"—we see Jesus on his Cross and we know that here God is overcoming real evil by means of his very much more real love. But God also surrounds us and invites us to be friends with him, through our daily choices and in our daily duties. In that way we can work with him and let ourselves be used by him—by our own glad and free consent—to put a stop to or to correct the "wrong-going" about which I have written. He forgives us when we "sin", integrating us once again into his ongoing plan for good. He lets us really help him.

'The evil in the world does not get completely out of hand. God's faithful action prevents that. And once evil happens, as it so obviously does—in the natural disasters which damage the world and men, in the pain which is found in the animal world, and in human suffering like your own—God ceaselessly strives to put all these ends and pieces together however stubborn and recalcitrant to his plan they may seem to be.

'You and I are Christians. That signifies that we believe that God's character and his way of doing things in the world is revealed to us in Jesus Christ. We believe that the clue to God's heart is there, in a human life completely given up to God's will and purpose. God *is* Love. His love is not soft or sentimental, as human love so often is. It is a love which identifies itself with the world and with men and women, even in their anguish over evil, in their personal suffering, in their death. It is a love which can demand great things because it is a love which always gives and gives and gives—a love which also yearns for response, so that God can rejoice in his children's loyalty and goodness, as they become true men and women, the wholesome and authentic personalities that he means us to be.

'To say that, however, is at the same time to say something else. It is to say that in Jesus we see into our own human nature as it really is intended to be—like Jesus, we are to be entirely given to God's will and purpose. Our truest manhood is placarded before us in Jesus, just as the heart of God is also placarded before us in him. You and I, and every man or woman or child who lives in this world, are being created to become personal, free, loving, instruments for God's love to work in and through. This is why we read in the New Testament that Christ is "the express Image of God", while the Old Testament tells us that we too are made "in God's image".

'In any specific instance of suffering, like yours, it is very hard to say how and why it has come about. We can only say that in a world like the one I have described, with human beings like ourselves who have some measure of freedom, all of us belonging together in what the Old Testament somewhere styles "one bundle of life", this suffering *does* happen, and *is* real. You know that well enough. Our Christian faith, building on a sound and intelligent interpretation of the world but adding to that interpretation its own unique conviction about Jesus Christ, teaches us that out of the very horror of pain we can become richer, finer, more devoted, more loving persons.

'Our faith helps us to "take it", because in the life of Jesus we see suffering and rejection and death, used to bring joy and acceptance and life in love to others. Our faith enables us to use what we know and see, above all what we feel, of suffering and rejection and death. We *might* face the situation angrily, filled with hate. But we can also face it with courage and confidence. Sometimes we can work with might and main to remedy evil or prevent its occurrence; God wants us to do that, if we have the chance. Sometimes we can do little or nothing, especially when we are ourselves caught up in anguish. But yet there is one thing we can all do: we can see that love shines through, "enduring all things" (as St Paul writes in First Corinthians 13) and emerging strong and victorious.

'Finally, as I bring this long letter to an end, let me say something else which I believe to be very important for people like us who rejoice in calling ourselves by the

Christian name. I must write this very carefully, because I do not want you to think for a moment that I am talking cheap and sentimental "piety". What I wish to say is this. Anybody who suffers can unite his own bit of pain, great or small, with the suffering of Jesus Christ and with the loving (and suffering) heart of God himself. We can offer our pain to God in Christ, as part of our total loving and free acceptance of God and his good purpose in the world. Jesus himself did just that, when he was faced with suffering and death. You remember how he offered himself to God, aligning his own will and desire with God: "Father, if it be possible, let this cup pass from me. Nevertheless, not my will but *thine be done.*"

'That was no passive acquiescence. In Jesus' words the stress should be put on the "thine" and then, even more strongly, on the "be done". *Thy* will *be done*—that is, be accomplished through my offering, my giving, my committing of myself to its being done.

'So, I suggest, we can say something like this: "I don't know just why this has happened to me, but I do know that it has happened and is happening. It is within God's world and he can make something out of it. I pray God to take this pain I endure *and* my enduring of it, to use it in his supreme wisdom for good purposes as he continues making his world, for the overcoming of evil and the achievement of greater good. This is *my* offering, united with Christ's loving offering of himself. Thank God that through Christ I can see that God is always doing better things than I or anybody else can see, pray for, even imagine. *He* does indeed "work all things together towards a good end, for those who love him".'

PART TWO

The Goodness

1

Taking Love Seriously

EVERY Christian of course know perfectly that love is a very significant religious criterion. But I think few of us understand that love also can be a theological criterion.

Every theology has got to have some starting point and some reference; and in traditional Christian thinking God as pure being, God as absolute mind, God as unconditioned will, perhaps even God as a 'ruthless moralist', to use a phrase of Professor Whitehead's, has been given this central place. It is my own conviction that such a procedure is entirely mistaken, and that it represents what I must call an apostasy on the part of Christian theology. *Love* must be taken with utmost seriousness as the final theological criterion, precisely as in our Christian thinking and doing we recognise that love is the basic religious criterion.

Of course the word love is a highly ambiguous word. There is the sort of love which is nothing but sentimentality. When I was young there was a play which I remember seeing on my ninth or tenth birthday. The title of it I have quite forgotten, but the point of the play was that if we were all very nice to one another the world would be a much happier place, which is doubtless the case; that if we loved one another everything would be very lovely indeed; in fact that love consisted in having kindly feelings towards other people. That is one way of interpreting the meaning of love, but it is, as I am sure we would all agree, a superficial way. Personally, and this may shock some people, I prefer the Hollywood version of love even if it is over-emphatic on the sexual, because at least in that version there is strong passion, enormous and urgent desire. But even love in the Hollywood style will not quite satisfy.

What we really want to talk about is a relationship which is characterised by tenderness, which works by persuasion rather than by coercion, which seeks mutuality or participation between the parties in question, in which there is intentional faithfulness or commitment, and that kind of hopefulness which Baron von Hügel once described as 'eager, tiptoe expectancy'. This is love as I understand it in the New Testament sense of the word. When in what for me is the greatest passage in the New Testament, the fourth chapter of the first epistle of St. John, we read that 'God is Love' and that 'His love is known to us in that he sent his Son', and that 'if we dwell in love we dwell in God and God in us', we can easily see that the intention of the writer is to stress an active, dynamic, living, concrete relationship marked by precisely that tenderness or persuasion, that mutuality and participation, that faithfulness and hopefulness which establish, between the parties concerned, the most intimate and real rapport that is conceivable. It is love of this sort that is the theological criterion; or so I think.

I have mentioned the name of Professor Alfred North Whitehead whose thinking for me represents the most important work in our century in the providing of a conceptuality or pattern of thought for the statement of Christian faith. Whitehead remarked at the end of his Gifford lectures, *Process and Reality*, that all too often the

model for God which has been employed in Christian
theology has been the 'ruling Caesar', the 'unmoved
mover' or the 'ruthless moralist', a phrase which I have
already quoted; and he suggested that there is another
model which has not been taken with that degree of
attention which its origin merits. It is the model, drawn
from what he calls the 'brief Galilean vision', of a love
which neither coerces nor rules by imperial dictate, which
as he says is a 'little oblivious of morals', which works with
tenderness; and which for him is the appropriate model
when we speak of God.

I shall say more about this in respect to its application
to God in the next chapter, but now we must think about
man. What is true in respect to God is also true in respect
to ourselves. How do we think of ourselves? What really
is man? The classical definition which St. Thomas
Aquinas took from Boethius, 'man is an individual substance of a rational nature', has its value of course. Man
does have reason, to a greater or less degree, although it is
worth noting that Aquinas' humanity asserted itself
when in describing man he added that he is 'animal
risibile', the laughing animal.

Some people of a more materialistic turn of mind would
say that man is nothing more than a complicated mech-
anism; he is hardly more than a computer who happens
to function in a singularly intensive way. Others would
think of man as a body, merely a body. He is perhaps a
more interesting and more sophisticated example of body
than, say, a pig or a dog, but a body he is, and whatever
else may be said about him is simply epiphenomenal,
incidental, like the smoke which used to come from the
railway locomotive, but which had nothing to do with
driving the engine.

There is also a very peculiarly spiritual view of man, which talks about him as a soul and thinks that his body is rather irrelevant. Indeed, in the words of the American folk-song, his body may 'lie mouldering in the grave, but his soul will go marching on'.

There is something doubtless in all of these definitions, but I propose taking the criterion of love with utmost seriousness. Man is best defined as a lover in the making. He is a lover compounded of body-mind with capacity to will, with strong desires, with all the apparatus that goes with it; but the *definition* of man is in terms of his capacity to love, to give love and to receive love. In the third chapter I shall say something more about this. Yet if man is a lover in the making, he is certainly a frustrated and disordered lover. He is frustrated because of the conditions of time and place, of circumstance, the limitations imposed by his bodily and mental equipment, so that he simply cannot love as he might wish; but he is also disordered as a lover. St. Augustine has a prayer in the *Confessions* in which he asks that God will 'order' his loving. He knew that so much of his urgent desire to give and to receive was misdirected. He loved the right things in the wrong way, or he loved the wrong things with a zeal that was not appropriate to such things, and he knew that he needed to have his loving put right. He needed, in fact, what in Christian theology we call by the word redemption. He needed the grace which would enable him to order his loving aright; and we shall speak about this in our fourth chapter.

But man, and I should say God too, precisely because of this quality of love and this capacity for love, requires community. Love is the opposite of self-centred individualism. God loves his world and man loves his brethren. We belong together in a bundle of life, so that we cannot live, much less love, unless there are others with whom we may be in mutuality tenderly, and per- suasively open to them and giving ourselves to them in the faithfulness and expectation which involve commitment and the trust that new things may happen among us.

Man is by nature a social animal, said Aristotle. It is worth noticing that in the *Nicomachean Ethics* the discussion leads up into the *Politics*; and the *Politics* means not only governmental arrangement but also social belonging, *Polis*, in Greek, is 'city'; for a Greek man was a citizen, a social being, and whatever else may be wrong with Aristotle (I think a great deal is wrong with him, and the Christian Church made a great mistake in the thirteenth century in attempting to re-state Christian thought in Aristotelian idiom), here at least Aristotle was right: man is a social being, naturally, by creation.

So it is not to be wondered at that in Christian under- standing man's sociality finds its expression in that fellowship of loving persons which we call the Church. The Church *is* fellowship. It is the relationship of persons living in love, love of the quality disclosed in the life of its Lord; and in our fifth chapter we must speak of this, the Church as a community of love.

Where does it all lead? What is the destiny before us? More opportunity to love. Whatever we may want to make of the symbols familiar to us in respect to the 'last things', they come down to saying that love is the only survival, precisely as love is the only meaning. William Morris once remarked that Heaven is fellowship, and absence of fellowship is Hell. I should phrase that slightly differently: to live truly in love is to live truly in God, and that is all we can mean by Heaven. To live without love is death, the absence of the love that is God, and this is Hell. To this we turn in our sixth and last chapter.

The recusant poet Robert Southwell has a sentence which I like to repeat: 'Not where I breathe, but where I love, I live'. It is not only because I believe so firmly that this is the theological criterion, that I would thus stress this centrality of love; it is also because in the apologetic task, where we endeavour to communicate the Christian gospel to our contemporaries, we find love a real point of communication. Talk about first cause, unmoved mover, necessary being, logical explanation, and dictator of moral principles, seems to mean little or nothing in a time impatient of metaphysical discussion and doubtful about moral ultimates in the form of codes or laws. But talk about love strikes home, for all men— every one everywhere—yearn for and need love. Love, giving and receiving in mutuality, with deep hope and with commitment of self, is what the world is seeking. And a gospel about love—love cosmic and divine, love local and human—speaks to our age. And not by accident either, since 'God *is* Love' and 'he who dwells in love dwells in God and God in him'.

2

God is Love

WHENEVER one meets a professed atheist the question to
ask him is, 'In what God do you not believe?' Because
atheism can be a most valuable theological enterprise.

There are models of God which no Christian ought to
believe and there are theological ideas of God which, as
I suggested earlier, bear very little relationship to the
central Christian affirmation that God is love. At no
time has this been made more clear than today, when there
is a rather vocal school of theological writers who call
themselves the 'death of God' theologians. What God is
it who is dead? And if one asks this question one dis-
covers, in fact, that it is not the death of *God* which is
being announced, but it is the *concept* of God as arbitrary
power, remote first cause, moral dictator, allowing no
room for the freedom of his creatures. This concept of
God has gone dead on these writers, as indeed it has gone
dead on a great many other people who have never
articulated the idea at all. If it were God's death that
were in view, my own feeling would be that expressed
by Mark Twain when a New York newspaper reported
that he had died in London where he was visiting. Mark
Twain commented to a reporter, 'The story is greatly
exaggerated'. But that certain concepts of God have gone
dead is apparent to all of us, even to parsons!

Now in working towards a viable concept of God, the
first thing that we ought to do is to look at the world

which we say God has made, although it would be more appropriate to say the world which God is making. If we look at the world, we see creation in process. We see things coming to be. And in that processive world we see everything in relationship to everything else, so that it is impossible to talk about completely insulated and utterly separable moments or instances. Everything is connected; and when the novelist E. M. Forster put on the title page of *Howard's End* the phrase, 'only connect', he was speaking perhaps more wisely than he knew.

Connection, interrelationship, penetration of one thing by another: this is the sort of world in which we live. It is a societal world. And if this be the case about the world, a world on the move, in which social relationships are crucial, it must also be the case in respect to God, because God cannot be conceived as the great exception to all those principles necessary to explain how the world is and goes. To think of him in such a way would be to make him irrelevant and utterly unrelated. Rather, he is the chief exemplification, in an eminent or supreme manner, of those principles in the world which show us how that world is going. That is to say, God is participant in process too, and God is supremely related. He is indeed the chief of all causes, although he is not the only cause, since creatures, too, may bring things to pass. But he is also the supreme effect; what happens in the creation influences him.

One of the mistakes of Christian theological speculation has been to deny, presumably for God's supposedly greater glory, what all Christian experience knows full well to be the case, namely that we do affect God, who rejoices or who suffers, who shares, who is enriched or deprived by what goes on in the creation. Otherwise we should deny in theory what we know in fact, that we count for God, and that God counts on us.

This view of God which sees him, not in splendid isolation from his world, but in intimate relationship with it, is simply a variation on the theme, God as love. No lover dwells in separation. No lover loves only in principle. No lover is self-contained. No lover is utterly self-existent, without contact. Nor is it possible to think of a creator who does not create, although some philosophical theologians have engaged in this impossible enterprise of thought. If God is Creator, as the first phrases of the creed would suggest, and as the entire biblical witness testifies, then he is always in the relationship of creator to creation. So creation is not some event in the past, but is a continuing activity in each present. Indeed creation might be described, in words of an old teacher of mine, by saying that 'God always lets things make themselves by the use of his creative power'.

Now if this conception of God is taken with serious attention, a great many of our doctrines will be seen in a new light. Let me speak of two or three by way of illustration. Providence is not the ordering of things round, but it is the inexhaustible capacity of creative love to use things aright, so that their best good may be accomplished. Omnipotence is not coercion, but it is love working to harmonise all other exercises of freedom. Omniscience is not complete knowledge of everything which has or has not happened, but it is a relationship in which there is awareness of what has occurred and what is occurring, with a grasp of all the relevant possibilities, but without imposing a decision on free creatures to whom God has given the right to make responsible choice. Omnipresence is not some odd idea of everything in

God by reason of exemplars or types of those things in creation. Rather, our analogy might be that of mind and body, where the awareness which we have is inclusive of the total organism, so that God might be described as like the mind in relationship to all the occurrences in the cosmos, included in his awareness, precisely as they are. The outstanding illustration of this changed approach is revelation, not as the disclosure of theological propositions, as if from on high God dropped down little pieces of paper, saying 'I am Trinity in Unity' or 'Jesus Christ is God/Man in one person', or 'Man is a sinner, and I redeem him by the act of Christ'. No, revelation is in event, in natural event and in historical event, in a processive and societal world where some moments are of crucial importance, disclosing with singular intensity what God is up to in his world. And then in consequence we may make statements, more or less adequate, in any case never fully satisfactory, about what has been disclosed.

In this cosmos, where in Hopkins' lovely phrase, 'there lives the dearest freshness deep down things', there come moments of recognition, as in our own experience, say, with one we love. There are points when we are enabled, by something the loved one does, to see more deeply than ever before or anywhere else what is the truth about that one's character and purpose and act. God is in the whole process as participant; thus the whole process is incarnational, and is an at-onement. But in the man Jesus, where love given and love received met as in a tight clasp of the hands, we Christians say, 'Here is the truth in act'. The Fourth Gospel tells us that truth is not something known speculatively by the mind: truth is done. In Jesus the truth is done in act. It is indeed, in Christopher

Smart's glorious phrase from the *Song of David*, 'determined, dared and done'. It is an accomplishment in which God, ceaselessly active, acts in singular intensity, and man, ceaselessly responsive to God, responds with equally singular intensity. But always God is Love-in-act. He is the cosmic lover. His love moves the sun and the other stars, but it also moves in men's hearts and lives.

We shall be seeing presently how God as love is known in man, the frustrated and disordered lover, but for the moment I should wish only to say that the doctrine of Atonement is illuminated by this conception of the living, dynamic God participant in a societal process.

We cannot think of God in commercial dealings with his creation. All those concepts of Atonement which speak in terms of bargains, or which use the idiom of the law-court or of ancient sacrificial rites, have gone dead on us today. We ought to have the imagination to recognise that for those who first used these images there was an evocative quality that made them meaningful. But for us this is no longer the case. Although there are doubtless some theologians living in the airless chambers of speculation who may still talk in this fashion, nothing is communicated. However, Atonement seen as the release of love, working like personal influence, deepening and quickening relationships, does mean something to our world today.

The abiding truth in *all* Atonement thought is something like this: from whatever threatens most to destroy human existence, God by Christ delivers men. We can see how the paradigm works out: if one thinks of demon-possession as the greatest threat, then the deliverer from the demons will be redeemer. If one thinks, with Athanasius, of mortality and corruption as the greatest threat, then the bringer of immortality and incorruption will be the redeemer. If one thinks of slavery as the greatest threat, then the one who frees from slavery will be the redeemer. If one thinks of inability to make adequate recompense for wrongs done (Anselm) as the greatest threat, then the one who bears the punishment that should be ours will be the redeemer. If one thinks, as we tend to do today, that the greatest threat to human existence is lovelessness and the loneliness which is its consequence, he who brings love and awakens the response of love and for loneliness supplies fellowship, will be the redeemer.

God is love, in loving relationship, always acting by love, luring, soliciting, inviting, persuading, willing, not against men's wills, but by the very power of love to convert wills; and I should say that such an approach meets most of the objections men make to ideas of God that are either sub-Christian or un-Christian—ideas that almost everybody today rejects, and, tragically, thinks that in rejecting these God himself is rejected. But no: in rejecting a lie one is moving towards acceptance of truth; and I suggest that much of the contemporary rejection of God is really a witness to the living God, the true God, the only God, whose nature and whose name, as Wesley said, is 'pure unbounded love'.

3

Man Made for Love

THROUGHOUT his history, once he became a thinking and puzzled being, man has been a problem to himself. Who is he? What is he here for, and where is he going? As we saw at the beginning, some people have been content to think of man as an intelligence who happens to possess a body, whilst others have thought of him as essentially a complicated instance of the animal world. But nobody who has really looked deeply into himself can be content with either of those ideas.

Nor can we be content with thinking of human nature as if it were static, given, already fixed. On some occasions I have spoken of the experience which so many have had when they were doing biology in school. They were presented with a cat, or perhaps a frog, and were told to dissect it. Having done this, they then drew on paper, with the use of various coloured crayons, a 'map' of the cat or the frog, showing what in biology is called its morphology. And that word is perhaps indicative of what in fact the exercise amounts to, because it is simply a formal pattern and it misses what is most important about either the cat or the frog, that these are living creatures. A dissected cat is a dead cat and a dissected frog is a dead frog.

So also, many of the descriptions which are made of human nature suggest that one is in fact talking about a dead man rather than the living, vibrant personality that we observe and that we know in ourselves. I suggest that it is best to think of man as a 'becoming'; to be a man is to be on the way to manhood. It is not to be an accomplished fact. In other words, there is a drive or a thrust or a dynamic in human nature which cannot be forgotten if we hope accurately to describe what it means to be human. This is a drive forward towards the fulfilment of possibilities—possibilities that are contributed by the past as it is remembered; and by the present relationships in which we stand, not only to others of our race but to the whole environing world, all of which plays its part in influencing us; and also by future possibilities that seem newly presented to us and whose fulfilment might bring the realisation of a better and richer manhood than is ours now.

If I were going to say what seems to me to be most distinctively human it would be neither rationality, important as that is, nor the drive of will, important as that is, but it would be man's urgent desire: his desire to become all that is in him to become in community with his fellow men. Man is a thrust of love who seeks fulfilment in loving and being loved, in giving and receiving, and this in richest community.

But of course, this is inclusive of the whole of his manhood; it is not just a spiritual striving; it is not just intellectual fulfilment. His body is involved too. In the biblical witness, nothing stands out more clearly than the unitary or organic conception of man, which for whatever reason the Jews so insistently held. Not for them the hellenistic idea of the body as the prison-house of the soul. Not for them the notion that we could escape from our physical organism into some cloud-cuckoo realm where we might dwell amongst eternal ideas. The very fact that they thought of resurrection of the body, once they came to think at all of this kind of matter, rather than of immortality of the soul, is indicative of the point.

The total personality in the making is body/mind, spirit/matter, soul/sense, and never the one without the other. Thus for the Jew to think of himself as an historical being meant not that he happened to occur in the course of the ongoing of events, but that he was rooted and grounded in the common stock of the creation, and all of him must be understood in relation to that creaturely status in the natural order. And this was incorporated into the primitive Christian anthropology, or thinking about man, which was thus Jewish in orientation. The importation of hellenistic ideas, (not even Platonic ideas really, but the current hellenistic dualism between mind and matter, soul and sense, reason and body) has brought about in Christian history the odd notion that man is essentially a pure spirit who happens for a time to inhabit a material body.

One of the most welcome events of the last two centuries has been the discovery, or the rediscovery, that we are organic to nature, and that there is no sharp split between man's material and man's spiritual existence. I have often quoted the French philosopher, Gabriel Marcel, who says that man does not *have* a body, he *is* a body. Thus, when I have a pain in my little toe, I say that *I* have the pain; I do not say that my little toe has the pain, but that *I do not*. Psychosomatic medicine is a splendid demonstration of this remarkable interrelationship of matter and mind, of body and soul.

Some may think it surprising that at once I go on to say that I believe another welcome event in more recent times is the re-discovery, especially by younger people (who thus often offend their elders!) that man is a sexual being. For a great many reasons, the history of which there is no point now to investigate, man's sexuality has been dismissed as irrelevant by far too many Christian thinkers.

Not long ago, in a bookshop in Cambridge, I bought a remarkable essay by Rosemary Haughton called *The Act of Love*. It is a study of faith. I was told by the manager that when he was reading back into his microphone for a recording of purchases the names of the books sold during the day, a lady customer of the shop, hearing him give the title of this book, remarked in a very sharp voice, 'So that's the kind of shop you are!' and walked out. Well, this lady showed two things: first of all, she had immediately identified the act of love with the sexual act; and this is a good thing to have done because the two *are* related. But she had also indicated that she regarded any such association of ideas as an horrific thing. And that is the tragedy of so much of our Christian history in respect to this aspect of human nature. Young people today, we are often told, are very much over-conscious of sexuality. I should have thought this was an eminently desirable reaction from the asexual picture of man that so often they find, or think they find, in Christian and conventional moral circles.

Man is a thrust of love. He is made to love, or better, he is being made so that he may become a lover. And all of him is involved in the process. Ultimately the goal of his loving is that cosmic love which 'will not let us go'. But because we are embodied creatures, we find most of what we know of love in, with, and under (the Lutheran prepositions for eucharistic presence) the love that we meet humanly speaking. It is too bad that the translators of the Latin collects in our prayer book, in this particular case perhaps Cranmer, did not include in the collect for the Sixth Sunday after Trinity the full Latin text, which speaks of our *amantes te in omnibus et supra omnia*, 'loving thee in all things and more than all things'. Instead, by the omission of the first phrase 'in all things', the suggestion is given that we can love God apart from the creaturely occasions in which he wills to be present and at work. But this denies the principle of incarnation, which asserts that God is known to us in, with, under the creatures, and only exceptionally apart from and in spite of the creatures.

It is fascinating to see how frequently in both Old and New Testaments the model of marriage or sexual love is used to describe man and his relationship with God; and it is highly significant that in the main stream of Christian thought, despite all the antagonism to sexuality and the substitution often of emasculated chastity for true charity, marriage yet has been understood as a sacrament, in which there are three partners not two: the man, the wife, and the love which binds them together, which is nothing else than God himself.

So also I should suggest that in all human relationships we are moving either towards this fulness in love, in which case we are becoming more human, or we are moving away from this, in which case we are denying our humanity. Even the professional celibate has not destroyed his human sexuality; he has channelled it in another direction from that which is common in our race. But if he sought to kill his sexual nature he would kill himself.

As a being moving towards fulfilment man requires his fellows. 'It is not good for man to be alone', and this participation with others is the chief way in which he comes to know God's most intimate nature. 'Pure, universal love, Thou art', said Charles Wesley; and how did Charles Wesley come to say it? By falling in love with love, as a popular song of a few years ago put it. He fell in love with God manifest in one of our own kind; and if we fear to put it in that way, we are afraid of being human and we are altogether too fearful about the dignity of God.

I think that if we wish to help our contemporaries understand their own nature we can often learn most from the songs sung by the Beatles and others. Whatever else one may say about the popular songs of the day they insist that love is greater than either of the partners in it; they insist that you 'can't earn' love; they insist that it is fulfilment; they know that we are only happy when we love. Most of all, they see the truth in that Spanish proverb, 'To make love is to declare one's sorrow'. They know the anguish as well as the joy of love. It is in our becoming lovers that we find the dignity and grandeur proper to man, to be a co-creator with God— fellow-worker, said St. Paul—in the creation of a situation where love is shared as widely as finitude will permit. If this is not the function of the Church, to provide such occasions and opportunities, I do not know what the Church is here for.

But the tragedy is that man, the lover in becoming, is frustrated by circumstance as well as by finitude. He must be selective in his loving. Only God is divinely promiscuous. And man is disordered in his loving, for alas! he does not know how to love aright.

4

Love Frustrated and Disordered

MAN who is made to be a lover finds himself frustrated in his loving and disordered in the expression of his love. This is a deliverance of human experience: frustration and disorder. The frustration of man as lover in the making is due very largely, if not entirely, to his finitude, to his place and time, to the conditions under which, inescapably, he must live. It is impossible for any one man to be aware of all other men. It is impossible to care as intensely for the human race as for this or that instance of it; and there are many other factors, both psychological and physical, which condition man in all that he does. He cannot jump out of his skin; he must recognise that he is a creature of time and place.

It would be wrong, I think, to hold men responsible for their frustration in loving when it is this sort of thing that one has in view, but it is not mistaken to hold men and to hold each man responsible for that disordering of our living which comes about by his free decision. Sometimes it is his own personal decision; often it is the decision of his ancestors or his associates, establishing a situation in which disorder in loving is inevitable.

Classical theology has spoken of 'original sin'—which is a not very happy phrase to describe an even less happy condition. The phrase is not happy because it appears to suggest that there is a kind of sin which is all about us and of which we are participant, which in and of itself is our personal responsibility. What the term means, as any classical theologian would know, is the origin of man's sinful state. Original sin means, in classical theology, the state in which human beings find themselves without or apart from that sort of engracement which enables them truly to realise their possibility as children of God; and the opposite of original sin (again in classical theology) is the state of grace.

Certainly the milieu which is ours is a milieu in which disordering is very easy, if not indeed inevitable; and for that milieu man is, in fact, responsible, although any individual man cannot be called responsible for that situation. I have often thought that original sin in its proper meaning should be interpreted sociologically, certainly not, as St. Augustine tended to do, biologically. And when people have remarked, after hearing me say this, that such a sociological interpretation does not take sin with sufficient seriousness or make it sufficiently an element in each man's personality, one could only reply that man's sociological belonging is as much himself as the cells of his body. We cannot live, we do not live, we are not, apart from our fellow men. We are naturally, by the fact of our creation, members one of another; and what is true of the society in which we live is true also of us, because we are social beings. So, the interpretation of original sin in a sociological way is no minimising of its reality, nor does it deny its integral relationship to each member of the race.

For all of us, then, there is a frustration largely due to our finitude, and a disordering due to our own decision or to our living in a milieu in which the decisions of others have so distorted the situation that the right choices are made, if at all, with the greatest difficulty. Unhappily but understandably, sin has been interpreted in most Christian moral theology in terms of violation of laws or codes or commandments, presumably enunciated from on high by the divine moralist. To say this is not to be quite just, because running through Christian moral theology there has always been another strand, in St. Augustine, for example. The real defect in man is in his loving; and I have already quoted the prayer in the *Confessions* where St. Augustine asks God to order his loves aright. Or, again, in St. Thomas Aquinas, in the *Secundum Secundae* of the *Summa Theologica*, where he discusses man as a moral being, the very heart of the law morally speaking is, in his own words, 'the spirit of charity in our hearts'. And certainly we know that in Luther the sense of violation of the purposes of a loving God was very central indeed to his awareness of himself as alienated and hence requiring redemption.

If in other moral theology one does not find references to sin as the breaking of some imposed law, code, or commandment, one sometimes finds it defined as the violation of the law of nature. This is a highly rationalistic concept. As commonly taught, it says that man by his reason is participant somehow in the eternal law which is God's good will for his creation, and that he can discern by rational insight the ways in which properly he should function as a human creature. For the most part, this is by observing the way things actually do go in realms such as the sexual life where sexual relationships lead, commonly, to the procreation of children. Hence it is a violation of the natural order of things to interfere with the common result of such intercourse; contraception therefore is sin. This natural law is the basis upon which in much Roman Catholic moral theology, until recently, the whole edifice of man's duty and of man's failure in duty has been built, although in quite recent times and in some Roman Catholic circles the situation is now very different.

St. Thomas Aquinas defines the ultimate deliverance of natural law very simply, and, I should say, unexceptionably: 'Do good, avoid evil'. But the difficulty is that there is no content there; and when he and most Roman Catholic moral theologians have proceeded, they have endeavoured to discover what is the good to be done and the evil to be avoided by looking at what I have called the way things commonly go. In other words, there is a tendency to confuse the order of nature in its observable sense with the ideal of man and the duty for man, which perhaps may not always be a matter for visible observation. But one would think that, taught as we have been by biblical studies concerning the origins of such sets of moral duty as the Ten Commandments, knowing as we do that a good deal of moral progress has in fact come precisely from our not following the ordinary processes which are observable in the natural order, one would want to find a better, certainly a more evangelical, understanding of the meaning of man's sin. And my own proposal is very simple: that sin consists in man's failure, by free decision, whether his own or that of the society in which he shares, to become really what in possibility he is made for. Thus, my sin is no infringement of an arbitrarily imposed law which has no relation to me. My sin, my violation of God's will, is in my failure to be truly a man. My friend Paul Lehmann in his fascinating and provocative book *Ethics in a Christian Context* has said that God's will for man is to make him and keep him human. This is exactly what I mean.

When I love the wrong thing or love the right thing in the wrong way, when that is to say, I am disordered in my loving, I am not authentically acting as I ought to act as a potential lover. I suggest that one might run through the list of sins commonly found in those ghastly little books for self-examination, and see that all of them which are of any significance can fall under this general rubric; although I must confess that some of the sins of which I was supposed to accuse myself when I was a pious little boy now seem to me to be so ridiculous that only persons lacking either in humour or common-sense could ever have included them in the list of sins. 'Have I laughed in church?' Thank God, yes. 'Have I crossed my legs while sitting in choir?'—and all the rest of the nonsense with which young people and others were encouraged to engage in what Baron von Hügel called 'a spiritual flea-hunt'. This is obviously absurd; but the serious sins can all of them be understood in terms of the disordering of my true capacity to love, to love God in and with my fellows, and to love my fellows under God.

Now if something like this is man's state, and if this state is a serious one, then serious remedies are in order. I interpolate here that those writers, of whom there have been several, who think that such an approach to the meaning of sin, found primarily in contemporary Roman Catholic moral theologians in France and Germany, and in a few instances (in not very clear form) in certain Anglican divines, lacks seriousness; those writers who think that such an approach diminishes the reality of sin and its grievous nature, are singularly impercipient. Indeed, to talk of sin in terms of love's violation by our disordering is to talk much more seriously than when one

talks of disobedience to this or that law. It was non-
Christian moralists who discerned that violation of negative
codes is very different from failure to live in positive terms
in obedience to true, loving demand; and one would have
thought that Christians would have had at least as much
discernment as non-Christian, indeed non-religious,
moralists.

Serious conditions require serious remedies, and the
Gospel, among other things, is remedy for sin. I say
'among other things' because I at least find it impossible
to accept that sin-centred or soterio-centric view, if I
may coin a word, which has dominated so much Western
moral theology, indeed all theology, especially since the
Reformation. The Eastern Orthodox have a more
wholesome and rounded view, I should say, understanding
that the Gospel includes much besides the remedy for sin.
It includes the completion of creation, the taking of the
world into the purposes of God, so that His splendour
may shine through it all. Sin, from our point of view, is
the most serious of all our problems, but it is not the only
thing with which the Gospel is concerned. Yet, among
other things, the Gospel speaks directly to man, sinner.
And the article of a standing or falling Church is justification by grace through faith.

Nobody can earn his way out of disorder. The Beatles
tell us that 'you can't buy love for money'. You cannot
order your loving by the payment of any amount of works
or good will. It is of grace. I am accepted, in the great
phrase of Tillich; and because I know that I am accepted
I can accept both myself and others. And being thus in a
condition of acceptability and acceptance I can begin
by sheer gratitude to re-order my love; or better, to let
the divine Lover teach me how to love aright.

5

The Community of Love

IN each of these chapters I have been trying to see how some specific aspect of Christian belief is illuminated if we take love seriously as our chief theological criterion: the doctrine of God, the doctrine of man, the doctrine of sin, now the doctrine of the Church, and finally human destiny and the meaning of human life.

We turn to the doctrine of the Church. If one looks at the Church, one is hardly inclined to call it the community of love. At least, many of our contemporaries would think of it as an association of like-minded people who think themselves better than most others and for some obscure reason find satisfaction in gathering together once a week for the purpose of mutual admiration. But despite the appearances, which, as so often, are deceptive, the Church is nothing other than the fellowship of those who, at least in principle, are caught up into the love of God in Christ Jesus their Lord, and aim to live one with another in such a relationship of love that they will contribute to the making present, in the world, of this love as man's authentic existence.

I have said that every occasion in the world is a strange complex event in which the past is remembered, not only mentally but viscerally; in which there are present relationships with others round about and with the total environment in which the occasion finds itself; and in which there is a thrust or movement towards the future with the hope that potentialities possessed by the occasion may come to rich fulfilment or satisfaction.

The Church may be seen in just this way. It has its memory. The memory is not only the consciously articulated theological doctrines, nor the obvious present liturgical practices, but a kind of corporate remembering of the event in history which brought it into being and of which the Gospels are a written record. The Church has its present relationships; it is set in the world and its concern is to be in closest contact with what is going on round it, influenced by the world which, as J. G. Davies has lately insisted, gives the Church its agenda; and also, please God, influencing the world round it so that more and more the world will reflect something of that divine charity which lives at the heart of the Church's existence.

The Church also has its subjective aim towards which it is directing itself. The biblical term for this is the kingdom of God, God's rule in the world in love; and the Church's purpose is to realise, through the working out of its own potential, the presence of that kingdom: And when I say 'realise' I do not mean simply 'be aware of' but I mean 'make real', bring into actual existence.

All the way through, the Church is a living entity. Almost everyone is prepared to use the New Testament phrase that the Church is 'the body of Christ'; but yet at the same time to think of the Church as more like an institution or an organisation or, at worst, a machine, fabricated by the Lord and working, after his departure, in some manner that is felt to be appropriate. This idea of the Church is found in one of the worst of our Victorian hymns: 'And though the Lord has gone, his Church remains below'. But surely, to take seriously the biblical image of 'body' means that we must understand the

Church as an organism, not an organisation; as a functioning, living, dynamic, vital movement, and not some mechanical apparatus. And if we do take this biological analogy seriously, although of course as Dr. Dillistone has rightly warned us not literally, we shall have to recognise that whilst organisations may be made, as an artisan can make some object, organisms grow. This has its bearing on reunion discussions, for organisms cannot be created *ad hoc* by committees appointed for the purpose. They must grow into their fulness; and this will mean living together, worshipping together, praying together, and I should say receiving the sacrament together, before we attempt institutional unity.

It is in this kind of context of the organic view of the Church—the Church as a living body with its memory, with its present relationships, and with its forward thrust— that we ought to see Christian worship and Christian service, and in particular, the meaning of ministry. Christian worship was in the early days of the Church entirely eucharistic, although the primitive Christians doubtless attended Temple services in Jerusalem and had their own meetings not unlike those of the synagogues for purposes of edification. But the *agape*, the love meal, was Christian worship. It is, I think, a most important fact of our time that Christians everywhere, of all denominational backgrounds and experiences, more and more are coming to understand that the Christian fellowship is both placarded as such and realises its identity as such when round the holy table eating and drinking together. Love incarnate becomes a fact and the disciples of Jesus are fed with the life which is love. This means, obviously, that the eucharist is a family meal and anything else we say about it must be said with this in mind. If it is sacrificial in nature it is the brokenness of life in love. If it is communion it is sharing in such life. If it is remembrance it is the memory of that love enmanned in our midst. If it is 'eschatological', an earnest of the kingdom of heaven, it is by anticipation of the reign of God in love. Such an approach, cutting underneath our familiar differences in eucharistic doctrine, can bring us to the place where we are ready to be made one in the feast of love, held by the community of lovers for the purpose of making real the love of God would have us manifest in His world.

Christian service or activity, our next point, is not the sort of thing which Father George Tyrrell, that tragic Roman Catholic modernist figure, once described as 'going about doing good, particularly the kind of doing good which involves a great deal of going about'. This misunderstanding seems to me very much a present fact. But Christian service is the implementation in concrete act of our being grasped by the love that 'will not let us go'. Because this is the case, the Christian in serving the brethren either within the community or outside it, is delivered from those anxieties which so seriously affect the case-worker, the social service agent, and many other well-meaning reformers. Observation makes clear, to me anyway, that there is always the danger of fatigue, of impatience, of a sense that one is not getting the response one expected. Perhaps one is mistaken; only God knows the value of what is being done. But at least for the Christian there is the assurance that it counts, because the Lord of love is in it and we are his faithful agents, who, in the famous words of St. Ignatius Loyola, 'do not ask for the rewards' which might obviously show that we were successful.

In the next chapter I shall say a little about some of those personal relations and some of those social concerns which are included in acting love, but for now I should simply wish to insist that what is done for love's sake may be a chore, but it is transfigured by glory.

Finally, in respect to ministry: the centrality of love in a picture of the Church as a living community with its memory, its relationships, and its striving to a goal, will provide us if we will have it so a rather different perspective from the usual one. All too often, it seems to me, for reasons that are historically quite understandable, the clergyman is considered as possessing a status which is his apart from anything that he does. I should wish to deny any such view of ministry, I should wish indeed to deny any theory which gives status of this sort to anybody or anything, because status is a term appropriate only in a static world. In a processive world function is more to the point. A thing *is* in what it does and in what it is becoming, rather than in some fixed posture which is there, and that's all one can say. So I should propose that in our thinking about ministry we should think of it in terms of what the minister is there to do, and not assume that by virtue of ordination, by what sometimes we call the grace of orders, he is the odd man out amongst his fellows.

What does a minister do? The memory, the relationships, and the aim of the Church are concepts that can apply to him, and for a very good reason, because the minister is the ministerial representative, as R. C. Moberly argued in his great book *Ministerial Priesthood*, for what the Church itself is all about; and one's view of the Church will determine the way in which one understands the ministry in the Church. Today our tragedy is that we have failed to relate these in an adequate way, so that whilst we think of the Church more and more as the living, dynamic community, the pilgrim Church which is the body of Christ as the servant of men, we still retain ideas of ministry which were appropriate only to a static conception of the Church, organisationally and institutionally conceived. If the Church remembers its past, the minister is the voice for that memory in the present world. He proclaims the Church's memory, its Gospel. If the Church is in relationship with contemporary men, the minister is the one who brings that relationship particularly to expression through his shepherding, pastoral, practical concerns. If the Church aims towards the bringing of the world into the kingdom where love reigns, the minister prophetically speaks of love as final criterion and final goal. Above all, if the Church expresses its life in love by a family meal where love is both celebrated and received, the minister is the appointed agent for the celebration and the communication of that love.

In this sort of way, what he is doing is being done not in separation from the life of the community but as its agent, and so all of his activity has as its point the realisation of the community's own existence, where love-in-action is seen at work in practical ways and God's children are enabled to become what God means them to be—lovers who find in him both their goal and their strength.

6

Growing in Love

I REMIND the reader that these chapters do not pretend to be comprehensive in nature. At best they are suggestive, at worst they are provocative. The purpose is to propose a way of looking at Christian beliefs which may illuminate them, both in respect to our own apprehension and in respect to the discipleship which is proper to every Christian. At no point, perhaps, is love so important to our thinking and our doing as when we are considering the meaning of Christian activity in the world. Such activity is twofold: first, and quite obviously, it is our behaviour and our concern for the promoting of those causes which will establish more widely the reign of love in the lives of men. But secondly, and as important, Christian action is that which goes on inside us as we seek to realise more fully the meaning of our manhood in and under God. Today perhaps, the latter aspect of Christian activity is very little regarded, and there is a danger to which I call attention and nothing more, of sheer *activismus* as a presumed synonym for activity. By this I mean the notion that if one is constantly on the move one has exhausted the meaning of discipleship. The difficulty here is that one would then have very little to contribute to a world which, as we all know, is very much on the move. If there were any justification needed, for what is commonly called Christian spirituality (a lamentably gnostic term), but what we might more appropriately call dedication and devotion in discipleship, it is precisely at this point.

Ralph Waldo Emerson, the American essayist, once remarked that of some people one could say that what they were spoke more loudly than what they said. Very often we assume that what we are is irrelevant both to what we say and to what we do, but this obviously is absurd. I shall not say anything more about personal devotion and dedication, but I must insist that the *activity* of a Christian as a lover can only be activity as *a lover* if love is permitted to grow in the inner man; hence personal prayer and all that is associated with it.

When it comes to action in the more obvious sense, love is like the Spirit in St. Paul's Corinthian correspondence: there are diversities of gifts, but the same love. Some people find themselves called to certain specific responsibilities as ways for the expression of their love. Baron von Hügel once said that love as a Christian understands it is caring; and every Christian must care, or as the Quakers would say, must have laid upon him concern for other men, which means as well the circumstances and conditions in which other men live. No man is a disembodied spirit, a pure intelligence, which is St. Thomas Aquinas's definition of an angel; and the attempt to deal with people as if they were disembodied spirits is both a denial of the incarnation as a principle and also sheer nonsense. But in this diversity of gifts different people will in fact feel care, show concern in ways that are appropriate to their own peculiar qualities, talents, and attractions. Yet the principle which is universal is the caring and the concern; nor does this mean necessarily membership on committees, an Anglo-Saxon substitute, often, for genuine love. Certainly it does not mean only what in inverted commas we call 'Church work', as if being a sidesman or a leader of the Girl Guides exhausted Christian discipleship.

Involvement in the world is for the Christian a corollary of God's involvement in the world, not only in his incarnate Son but in the whole of creation. The world matters to God because he loves it, and it affects God because a lover is always affected by that which he loves. So too with us. Of course, something of the sort is true of all men, by virtue of their creation, but the distinctive thing about the Christian is that he is a lover who claims to know why he loves, what to love, and how to love aright by the enabling grace of God as love.

The question in respect to any particular aspect of human relationships is never 'Where am I at this particular point?' but 'In what direction am I going?' Life is processive, and one can only understand it when one sees the movement towards goals. God judges us so, we should judge others so, and even think of ourselves so; in our personal relationships, obviously; in respect to social concerns, equally.

Some kind of participation in the ongoing struggle for racial understanding, industrial understanding, class understanding, national and international understanding, surely is incumbent upon us, not only because justice is a minimum necessity for human life which will be a real possibility without destruction, devastation, decay, but because justice is a way in which love expresses itself in the orders of society. Yet this world is not now, and seems hardly likely soon to become, the kingdom of God where love rules in all things. We are not yet there, although we are on the way (St. Augustine says *in via ad patriam*) and also even now participant in what the New Testament calls 'the powers of the age to come', which means, surely, 'Here, now, God is with us and in us as well as for us, as we seek to be fellow-workers with Him in the on-going creation'.

This is our manhood in its dignity. God does not treat us now as children who run to daddy whenever the going is hard and who are thus relieved of all responsibility. He treats us, as St. Paul himself says, as men. Here is the insight of Dietrich Bonhoeffer, so often misinterpreted. The great German martyr was not foolish enough to think that man has come of age in the sense of full and complete maturity, but he was Christian enough to believe that God treats us as sons and not as little babies.

To grow in love and in the acts of love is our Christian discipleship. Where does it lead? It leads to God himself. I have already said that God is not only the chief, although not the sole, causal principle, but is also the supreme affect who receives into himself all that is good, or that may be made to serve good, turning even the wrath of man to his praise. In God's concrete, consequent nature, to use Whitehead's phrase, all achieved good is received, to his satisfaction and for his further use in the accomplishing of love's purposes.

There may be evil which is irreducible and irredeemable. Is there any such? We do not know—it would be presumptuous for us to assume there is, when we consider what God did with the blackest of all deeds, namely Calvary's cross. But if there is irreducible and irredeemable evil as a surd in the cosmic equation, this certainly cannot be received into God's affective nature. It must be rejected, or in the idiom I should use, negatively prehended. Yet it is my own deepest faith that there is no such evil, since I am convinced that God's love is so strong that in the end it will hold all things captive, not by coercion, but by its loveliness.

Now how are we to conceive of human destiny in terms such as these? I suggest that we take with more seriousness than we are wont to do the Old Testament idea of God as remembering: 'Remember, O Lord, what thou hast wrought in us', 'Remember for good, O God, that which we have done', 'Remember thy servant, O Lord, according to thy loving favour'. God remembers, and nothing could be more real than the divine memory. This conception, to my mind, lifts out of its absurdity much that is said concerning human immortality.

If God remembers us for good, and can use what we have done and what we are for good, that is our immortality. Whether this includes self-conscious awareness of the fact, on our part, seems to me a secondary matter. We are permitted to hope that it is so. Does not a collect speak of 'a holy and religious hope', rather than speak in terms of complete certainty as if what we call life beyond death were a matter of demonstration? Hope we are permitted to have, provided we do not selfishly claim such persisting awareness as our due, and thus play dog-in-manger to the universe. All is *ad majorem gloriam dei*, which is to say, to greater love and wider loving, for God's glory is his love disclosed. It ought to be enough for the certitude of faith to say that through all the perishing of occasions love is the only certain survival, grounded and preserved in the love that is God. That is the promise and victory of faith; and so far as I am concerned or you are concerned, as self-conscious individual centres, can we not leave this with God, with whom in any event, whether we like it or not, it does remain? 'And with him be the rest.'